G000097410

# ★ The ★
# RORY'S
# STORIES

## LOCKDOWN LOOKBACK

**Rory O'Connor** is a stand-up comedian and mental health advocate. He is the man behind the phenomenally successful Facebook page *Rory's Stories*. From its modest beginnings, where Rory would share anecdotes, skits and observations about life as a GAA supporter, *Rory's Stories* is today one of the biggest social media pages in Ireland with 1.2 million fans. Rory has toured his material to sold-out audiences as far afield as Australia and the Middle East. He has published three bestselling books with Gill Books, including his memoir, *Rory's Story*.

★ **The** ★

# RORY'S STORIES

## LOCKDOWN LOOKBACK

## Rory O'Connor

Gill Books

Gill Books
Hume Avenue
Park West
Dublin 12
www.gillbooks.ie

Gill Books is an imprint of M.H. Gill & Co.

Designed by Síofra Murphy
Edited by Neil Burkey
Proofread by Djinn von Noorden
Printed by CPI Group (UK) Ltd, Croydon, CR0 4YY

This book is typeset in Minion Pro 12/18 pt.

*The paper used in this book comes from the wood pulp of
sustainably managed forests.*

A CIP catalogue record for this book is available from the
British Library.

5 4 3 2 1

# Acknowledgements

I would like to thank the public for their brilliant Irish wit under a Facebook post I made about life under lockdown, which is what inspired me to write this book. I would also like to give a special thanks to all the front-line workers who were incredible during the pandemic and to anyone who lost a loved one during those dark days.

Thanks to all the team at Gill for their help once again, to Jen Murphy for her brilliant illustrations, and to my family, who always back me in everything I do.

I hope this book gave you all a laugh or made you smile to yourself, because at the end of the day, humour is medicine for our mind and soul.

# Contents

## Chapter 2: Home and Family Life

## Chapter 3: Social Life (Or Lack Thereof)

# Preface

# Preface

I had planned to write another book down the road, but I certainly didn't think I'd be writing a book about a pandemic or a virus that stopped the world moving!

The idea came to me after I posted on my *Rory's Stories* Facebook page on the evening when most restrictions were finally being removed, saying, 'To think back to the days when ya couldn't go further than 2km from your gaff, guards everywhere asking where ya going, queueing up to do your food shopping, burning your hands with sanitiser and starting to think Guinness tastes nice from a can. We're in some place now!' It was just a few throwaway words, but what happened next led to the inspiration for this book. Talk about gathering momentum!

Everyone and anyone was posting comments under the post, talking about their various experiences of lockdowns, and some of them were absolutely comical. The post gave so many people such a laugh, and it hadn't been easy to laugh about what had just happened in the world! So the laughs led me to write this book. I hope you enjoy it, and that it brings back some funny memories of a crazy time in all our lives. In the book I share some of my own experiences during these 'mad' times, which included moving my family back into my parents' house to save for a mortgage (in the middle of a pandemic!), my wife falling pregnant with our third child (Lockdown Lucy) and also being lucky enough to move into our own home, all during the mad years of 2020 and 2021. There are also some stories from the public that are too unbelievable to have been made up! I promise that the one thing you will take from this book is that we Irish are simply unique.

# Chapter 1:
# Rules, Rules,
# Rules

# The start

In the early part of 2020, nobody could have predicted what was ahead of us, not just us in little old Ireland, but the whole world. You'd hear on the news about China and this 'coronavirus', but I, like probably a lot of Irish people, wasn't really paying any attention to it. Funnily enough, my daughter Ella would be listening when the news was on and maybe she had a sixth sense of what was heading our way! Once it started spreading in Italy, we knew that it was dangerous, and when the Italians started planning a lockdown to curb it, that's when my ears properly pricked up.

Fast-forward to around mid-February, and the first case of Covid was confirmed on the island of Ireland. 'Oh shit,' a lot of us thought, but again we still could not foresee what was coming our way. For me, it really started to hit the fan on 12 March, when it was announced that schools were closing because of this virus. I certainly don't remember schools ever closing for such a reason, so it was all starting to go belly up now. Then, when they cancelled the St

Paddy's Day parade, and when the then Taoiseach Leo Varadkar told us all to stay in our houses and keep away from others was when this nightmare started to get very real.

Myself, my wife Emma and our two children, Ella and Zach, moved in with my parents in December 2019 for a year to try to save for a mortgage. We had been renting a house in Ashbourne for seven years, but our landlord was selling the house and, with rent increasing, we said that it was time to bite the bullet and try to get our own house.

Moving back in with your parents at any stage is not easy. Now don't get me wrong, they were so good and supportive to allow us to move back in, especially with two young children, including a wild toddler. But Holy God, such a year to pick – the year of a once-in-a-lifetime pandemic, where for long periods nobody could go any further than 2km from their houses. I had had visions of Emma and me heading off on weekends away and leaving the kids with the built-in babysitters, but nope, it was going to be a nice, cosy house for the bulk of 2020.

But there were plenty of positives, no doubt. One was going back to the glory days of my mother's home cooking and washing. Hard to bate that!

# The early days

But to go back to where we were all at in mid-March 2020, it definitely was a scary and weird time for most people. When the first lockdown was announced we all believed (well, I did anyway) that we would just have to be very well behaved for a few weeks and that would be it. And most people were, to be fair. Talk about washing your hands until you reach the bone! I never washed me hands as much. And I remember there were even ads on the TV showing us how to wash our hands correctly, like what the actual fuck, when you think about it: fully grown adults learning how to wash our hands! And don't get me started on the hand sanitiser, or should I say 'gold dust'. Very hard to get the stuff anywhere – and the *price* of it! Whoever had a slice of that pie must have made a fortune. I wouldn't mind but it would burn the hands off you with too much of it, flat out putting the stuff on the poor paws no matter where you went.

# Whispers and WhatsApps

The old saying goes, 'Do you want the truth, or do you want a good story?' As Irish people, we love a good yarn, and the rumours and pure waffle were on another level at the start of the pandemic. Twenty years ago, rumours would have travelled by word of mouth or maybe a forum on a website, but not these days! Rumours can spread like wildfire in this day and age due to technology, especially WhatsApp messages. Do you remember some of the stuff that was sent around terrifying people? Some of the top-end ones I heard and got over WhatsApp were:

*My mam's hairdresser said that her neighbour has a friend she went to college with, who told her that the person who minds her dog when she is away on holidays said that at 12 a.m. today the Irish army will be marching the streets.*

*Lads, keep this to yourselves, but my mate was telling me that they are digging loads of graves around the country at the minute in preparation for all the people who will be dead in the next two weeks with this coronavirus. I know this for a fact because my mate's dad went to school with a man who used to drink in the Gravediggers in Glasnevin and only the best gravediggers drink there and he said a WhatsApp leaked from the gravediggers' 'Don't forget your shovel, lads' special WhatsApp group, and it pretty much said, 'Calling on every man who has ever dug a grave to come out of retirement and help us dig these graves.' So keep safe lads. Wash your hands and stay in your bedrooms. This shite is getting real!*

*Well folks. Have yas seen these messages? [screenshots included] I've a friend in the army and he sent them on to me. They have been told to be on O'Connell St at 6 a.m. tomorrow morning with their bags packed, ready not to be home for a week. They have to pack all their wet gear, dry gear, torch, compass, lights, bells, whistles, everything. He said there has never been more preparation for anything in the history of the Irish army. Scary times. Stay safe!*

*How's things? I just got sent this WhatsApp by a mate of mine who works in Centra, and they have been told that the company that makes cans of Heineken have run out of aluminium, so they just got their last few crates of cans into the shop there now! So get to all off-licences, as there will be no more cans of Heineken in the country by the weekend.*

*Wait till yas hear this – so ya know my old mate Dermo? Well, I haven't heard from him since we did phase two FÁS together. Well, he randomly sent me a text today saying that his da's mate works for Diageo, and they have been told that from 3 p.m. tomorrow until 9 p.m. every pub in the country will be open and it will be a free bar, because they want to get rid of all the drink before the country is locked down, as it's going off anyway. Now don't tell too many people this. In fact tell fucking nobody, cause otherwise the boozer will be wedged and we'll be left with just pints of scuttery Tuborg! I'll see yas at the pub no later than 1.30 p.m., because there'll be a massive queue outside once word spreads. Anyways, see yas there, men. We have one big last session left before lockdown!*

You see, with the power of WhatsApp, these messages could be (defo are!) made up by one person at home who's bored and sends it on to their mate, then their mate forwards it to a big WhatsApp group, and then it moves quicker than lightning! Then, just like that, half the country is shitting themselves over rumours! As the old saying goes, take everything you hear with a pinch of salt, especially in Ireland!

## Stories from the public

*My brother-in-law had just come back from Italy when Covid cases were starting over there. He then had a cough, so rang the HSE to be on the safe side. Not long after, an ambulance came with people in hazmat suits to test him. People were standing outside, taking pictures of him, putting it all over Facebook saying, 'Coronavirus is now in Waterford!'*

*Turns out he just had a cold.*

*(Roisin G.)*

★

*Remember the report on the news a few months into the first lockdown? A man coming home from Australia, and his parents came up from Leitrim to collect him with a horse box. Transported the son home from Dublin Airport to Leitrim in the horse box.*

*(Seamus K.)*

*Staying in my partner's mother's house over Covid. We had to dip our feet into a basin of bleach at the front door before going into the house in case our soles were full of Covid. She had heard on the news the French were doing it. It was like a hybrid between Covid and foot-and-mouth disease.*

*(Mary C.)*

*Some people were very cautious when it came to wearing a mask. I was driving through Westport at 1 a.m. of a Sunday morning and there was a young guy stumbling along a footpath barely able to stay on it, but fair dues to him he had a mask on. There wasn't a sinner for half a mile either side of him.*

*(Majella T.)*

*I went into Dunnes Stores at the start of the pandemic, and as I was walking down the shop floor I could hear, 'Excuse me, sir. Excuse me, sir!' I turned, and the security guard says, 'You came in the wrong door, that's exit only.' My reply: 'OK, lad.' His reply: 'Sir, please walk out and come in the proper door.' My reply: 'Would ya get ta fuck!'*

(Noel N.)

*Fell off my bike one day and a lady crossed to the opposite side of the road to shout over to me whether I was OK. I wouldn't have wanted to be dying, like.*

(Billy D.)

# Another level

We had various levels of restrictions during the pandemic. You had Level 5, which was basically full lockdown: only go to work if essential, only travel if essential, all pubs and restaurants only doing takeaway, only go outside your 5km if essential, etc. Well, it was Level 3 that made me scratch my head. Many decisions that were made during the pandemic made way for a lot of head-scratching, but Level 3 took the biscuit – the 'stay in your own county' restriction!

I live in Co. Meath, which is a big aul county. From, say, Ashbourne to Ballinabrackey (which is on the Offaly border), it's the guts of an hour's drive. Well, I can technically walk to Dublin from my own

house. A place called Ballymadun is just inside the Dublin border, and it's the parish where Dublin footballers Barney and Dean Rock live. In theory, I wasn't allowed to walk by their house, as it's over the border into another county, but I could get in my car and drive to Ballinabrackey, or Oldcastle on the Cavan border, or Duleek, which is on the Louth border. It made absolutely no sense!

Plenty of the auld Dubs broke this rule for an odd pint, and I don't blame them. When the pubs were closed in Dublin, they used to take the DART out to Bray for a dip, a 99 and a few pints. Sure, during the best of times you'd be doing well to separate the Dubs and the Wicklow heads out in Bray, so lockdown was no different.

I can imagine the Garda checkpoint on the Bray border:

'Where are you off to, sir?'

'Ah, I'm just heading home from work, officer.'

'I see, and do you usually go to work in a tank top, flowery Penneys shorts and flip-flops, with a pumped-up lilo strapped to your roof?'

'Ah, I'm only messing, Mr Guard. I live out in Bray. I'm just heading home.'

'I'd say you live out in Bray, alright. Could you name three other towns in Wicklow?'

'No bother. You have Wicklow, Courtown … and Butlin's! Can I go now, officer? I'll be late for the dinner!'

'Off you go, ya chancer!'

There were loads of people who had second 'homes' down the country. And the second home could be a house, a mobile home, a caravan – or a tent! When the restrictions were coming into effect, they would pack the bags and be gone, driving through the dark night heading for their location, and would be there nice and cosy by the time the restrictions came into play. A family from Clontarf one day could be a family from Rosslare the next morning. The Dubs would be working hard on their Wexford accents on the way down in the car overnight: 'If you hold your nose and speak, you'll sound like you're from Wexford, so everyone start practising that now before we run into a checkpoint! Say the word "quare" to the guard if we're stopped, and drop "The smell of rage off ya" into conversation. No, don't say that to the guard – maybe say it to your mother! And say you love strawberries. We should pass as Wexford people then.'

## Stories from the public

*When people were trying to keep the two-metre rule while out walking, instead of passing you on the footpath they would walk out onto the middle of the road to avoid you. Apparently, you couldn't get hit by a car during Covid.*

*(Paddy O.)*

*The hubby and me were standing apart in the queue for the supermarket because you were only allowed in on your own. We were going in with a trolley each and walking past each other like strangers.*

*(Alison L.)*

*I had to renew my truck licence so rang my GP to do my eyesight test. He made me do the test by looking through my car window in a car park in front of a load of people in their cars. I couldn't even see the letters and he couldn't hear me anyway. Still passed though!*

*(Stephen O.)*

*I had to go to hospital to get physio, but they didn't allow me inside, so I was in the hospital car park looking in the window on the phone to the girl who was explaining what I had to do, and it started raining so she told me to go back in my car – and I did the exercises sitting in the back seat of the car like a tool!*

*(Frank M.)*

*In the sports shop in my local town up until lately you could only try on one runner. They wouldn't get you the second runner to try on 'due to restrictions'. Was 'rona in the left foot or something?*

*(Bridget C.)*

*My mother's friend has a son who is a priest. When there was no Mass, he came to do a 'secret Mass'. They did it in the back room with the curtains down so the neighbours couldn't see them.*

*(Niamh M.)*

*I snuck down to Cork to buy a dog. Brought my mam's death cert with me in case I was stopped so we could say we were visiting her grave. Even had flowers 'for the grave' in my car. I gave them to the breeder, who was delighted! My mam would be very proud of me.*

(Sandra H.)

# The 2km rule

When they introduced the 2km rule it really felt like lockdown. I think everyone became so sick of looking at the same scenery every single day. Even when you went for a walk, you nearly always walked by the same people in the same places in your community, as most people had a routine during them days. It was probably the only way to keep yourself sane. I suppose for anyone who would suffer with their mental health, this was an extremely tough time. It was the whole unknown of it all that people struggled with. There was no guarantee of an end to this, and that's what had people feeling very low, anxious and worried.

I, for one, would very much be a people person. I enjoy chatting with people each and every day. I grew up on a housing estate, so I was used to leaving the house and talking to people all around me, and that just calmed down during the lockdowns. Well, a lot of people felt uncomfortable leaving their houses and avoided others when they were out, and some were reluctant to stop and talk for too long. When we did go on our family walk, myself, Emma, Ella and Zach would generally do the same loop, which took us about 45 minutes. Zach was a Curious George of a toddler, so we had to have him on a strap because we were afraid if he touched anything he might bring the virus back home to my parents. So walks with him were comedy in itself. I had to pull him back from touching anything, whether it be other people or objects. Kids weren't really allowed in shops during that time, but I had no choice but to bring him in with me. When I would have him alone, now that was carnage: him screaming to get out of my hands and head for the sweet counter and me trying to calm him down, while all along knowing children were not supposed to be in shops. Utter hardship! The minute we would come in the door, I would be scrubbing his hands and then mine.

Looking back, it was defo OTT, but that's the way it was during them times.

I suppose with living under my parents' roof we did have that extra bit of fear when we were out, because we worried about bringing the virus into the house. We were told to look after the old and vulnerable. Now to be fair, my parents are not that old. (Well, in their eyes, anyway.) But still, in them early lockdown days nobody knew what way this virus was going to go or spread. It just seemed that bit more dangerous, and once you heard of people getting very sick with it and dying, it certainly brought a different type of fear. You'd have to laugh, though, out on your daily walks, with the different types of people you would come across.

You had the 'normal people' – I can't think of any better term – who would just be out walking, not afraid to stop for a quick chat, keeping the two metres apart, no handshaking or hugging. Then you had the 'fairly paranoid people' with about four masks on them, and you can see by their eyes that they do not want to make contact with you. In fact, they would walk out onto a busy road just to avoid you!

I remember one day being out for our daily walk and we were coming down the back of my old secondary school in Ashbourne, where there's a little footpath with bushes either side of it. There is defo enough room for two people to pass each other without the worry of hugging and kissing. Well, one day we turned the corner and there was a man coming up towards us, wearing a mask, a scarf over the mask and his jacket zipped up.

I actually said to myself, 'This fella must have the virus, he just needs to get out of his house before he loses his marbles.' Unfortunately for him, we had just let Zach 'off his leash' to run down the hill, and as Zach made his way down the hill towards this man, the poor fella absolutely shat himself! With cat-like reflexes, he leapt about four feet into the air over a fence and stood there not willing to even make eye contact with any of us. It was as if he thought he had suddenly become invisible! He was rattling behind the fence. Keeping two metres away from him? We were about two acres away from the fella!

As we walked by him, I said, 'Are you OK, sir?' and, as God is my judge, he didn't even flinch, he just stared straight into the distance with his two hands out like he was trying to keep his balance, like some sort of ninja. I just said, 'Mind yourself, boss,' and walked on. I looked back at him, and as soon as we were a good bit away from him, he leapt back over the fence and sprinted off. I reckon he ran straight home and locked the door! It was both hilarious and sad at the same time that people were so afraid of this virus. I'm yet to see the man since. Mind you, he had so much protection over his face I probably wouldn't recognise him if he walked past me again, poor divil. I hope he's in better form these days!

## Stories from the public

*Trying to drive into the Phoenix Park to park up and go for a walk because it was within our 5km from home. We come to a checkpoint and the guard says, 'Where are yas off to?'*

*'Oh, just in for a walk around and bit of fresh air as well.'*

*I'll never forget his reply as long as I live. He told us to go home and stick our heads out the window.*

*(Lauren B.)*

*Going outside the 2km felt like a covert mission. We'd take all the small back roads, like everyone*

*else. Never met so many cars on those small winding roads to get to the forest for a walk. You'd hear tales of Mary down the road who was turned back. Then you'd get to the place and meet all your neighbours while out walking. The greeting was always the same:*

*'Hi Mary. If anyone asks, you haven't seen me here.'*

*We thought we were hilarious.*

*(Lauren F.)*

★

*My mam was breaking the 5km rule to visit her parents' grave. She came across a Garda checkpoint:*

*Garda: 'Where are you going?'*

*Mam: 'I'm going mad!'*

*Garda: 'On ya go, so.'*

*(Louise M.)*

★

*We broke the 5km radius rule and drove to Laytown Beach – best day ever – and smashed it with ice cream on the way home for the three kids. It was my one-year-old's first-ever 99 and my three-year-old twins were just delighted with life. But then there was a checkpoint ahead of us and my husband began shouting, 'Hide the ice cream! Hide it, they'll know we're not locals!' My twins tried so hard to demolish it but had brain freeze, and my one-year-old was like Father Jack and his drink. Rolled the window down, the guard took one look at the kids with evidence of ice-cream consumption all over their faces and the one-year-old getting locked on sugar. Fair play, the guard just asked the question and answered it himself: 'You're going home, aren't you?' He let us go. Cue me laughing for 15 minutes straight. It was like trying to get past bouncers and your mates are absolutely legless.*

*(Sarah Jane O.)*

*First time driving outside my 2km zone to get to Aldi and I get stopped by the guards:*

*Him: 'Where are you going, madam?'*

*Me: 'To Aldi, Guard.'*

Him: 'Are you looking for something in particular?'

Me: 'A fire pit, Guard.'

Him: 'I wouldn't bother, love, you're the 20th car I've stopped looking for the same thing.'

And yup, they were all sold out!

(Susan S.)

I live in Co. Wexford close to the Wicklow border and wanted to go for a spin one Sunday so we packed bags in the house full of non-perishable foods and put them in the boot of the car so, if stopped by the Gardaí, we could say we were grocery shopping. The only catch was that we were driving past the 5km radius to a village that didn't have any shops, so our story was that we got groceries in Gorey and were bringing them to our elderly relative in Co. Wicklow. Bags of nerves we were, and the added guilt when we stopped at a Centra to get a coffee, knocking it back and throwing the cups away in case we were caught with our 'non-essential' indulging.

(Grainne B.)

*I was out walking in a forest that was 6km from my house when there was a 2km limit. I was heading back to my car after my walk and had to hide. Cops were patrolling the car park handing out fines, so I hid behind a tree and warned fellow oncoming law-breaking felons to hide too.*

*(Nicola C.)*

# Covid and curtain-twitchers

One thing I couldn't get my head around during the pandemic was the stigma in relation to actually getting or having Covid. Especially in the early days, when not that many people had Covid, in every parish all over Ireland there were whispers about who had it. It nearly felt like the plague. I thought it was very unfair. In housing estates, if you saw a delivery van or someone pull up outside the house and leave shopping at it, there were all the curtain-twitchers looking out the windows: 'Ah yeah, I told you the McGowans have the Covid, didn't I? Didn't I?

Wonder now where they got that from ...' and all these silly rumours would be floating around. God forbid if someone walked out into their garden when they had Covid – the neighbours would all be on a mad one giving out.

## Stories from the public

*Looking at the sky in the stillness of the day, staring at the jet stream of a plane in awe – 'They're either going for PPE to China or coming back with it.'*

*(Fiona M.)*

*Called in to my elderly parents in pre-mask times to drop shopping in and collect something from the kitchen. My dad wrapped a tea towel around my mam's head in case I passed the virus on to her as I whizzed past.*

*(Gillian C.)*

*My poor husband got Covid in 2020, and because myself and the kids were negative, he decided to stay in the caravan in the front garden. I used*

*to bring his meals out to him and pass them in through the window.*

*My neighbour noticed and was giving me dirty looks for days. One day he knocks on the caravan and says to my husband, 'Did she kick you out, lad? You can stay in mine till you're sorted!'*

*My husband laughed and says, 'No, I have Covid, and they don't, so I'm just quarantining in here!'*

*Poor neighbour says, 'Ah OK, haha, I thought you were in the dog house!' Then his face drops and he nearly breaks his neck tripping over himself to get away from the caravan in case he catches anything.*

*(Naomi K.)*

# The news bulletin

When we were living in my parents' house during the first big lockdown we would have our dinner at the same time most evenings, about 5.30 p.m., and once the news came on there would be silence at the dinner table and up went the volume, nearly craving the bad news! One thing that us Irish seem to enjoy, well certainly the older generation anyway, is a bit of bad news! *C'mon, hit me with the bad news, hit me!* Like, I would have never watched the news pre-pandemic, unless something big had happened in the country or around the world, but other than that, no interest. I had the mindset that if it was important enough news, someone would tell me. I always associated the news with negativity, so why would I watch it? Plus, social media is there all day long, and if anything is going down you will see it there fairly quickly. It's not always spot-on true, but the bones of it will be found there.

I've been saying it for a long time now, but why doesn't each news bulletin finish with a positive piece or story? There is loads of negativity out there if you want it, but there is also plenty of positive news out there as well – people getting the all-clear from cancer, a miracle pregnancy, a close call with death or a good deed. Like, it doesn't have to be anything incredible. Just a simple little bit of positivity and a giggle to end the news. Leave people with a sense of goodwill and hope! Sure, if you're stuck, just have a look on Facebook and read the status that Mick from Mullingar posted:

*Jaysus, lads, I woke up this morning with a brutal
hangover from my best mate's 21st birthday, some
session! But to my delight, I picked up my jeans off
the floor and found a crumpled-up €50 note in the
arse pocket. Happy days, off I go now to get a nice
fry-up. Hope your day started off as good as mine
– Yeowww!*

Send a TV camera down to interview Mick,
because it's just all too doom and gloom! Sure, we
have all found a few bob in our jeans after a night
out over the years. It's a positive story and everyone
can relate to it. Especially during the pandemic, the
positive news was badly needed to end a bulletin,
because we would be sitting there in the kitchen with
half the dinner ate and the news on full blast to hear
how many people now had Covid and how many
poor unfortunate people had lost their lives to this
horrible virus.

My mother even had a Covid diary she kept in the
house, and every day she would take it out and write
down how many cases, deaths and where they were
in the country! Not just in which county, but village
and town too! She might as well have been working
for RTÉ or Virgin Media! I found this bonkers, like
c'mon, Ma, things are depressing enough and there

you are writing down all the figures to look at each day and remind yourself how poxy the times are we currently live in.

But that's an Irish mentality for you – hit me with the bit of bad news so I can ring Mary and tell her, and then she has some bad news to ring Pauline about. It's an Irish domino effect!

# Garda checkpoints

Garda checkpoints – where do I even start with this? For me, pre-pandemic Garda checkpoints were to check your tax and insurance, make sure you had no drink taken behind the wheel and on a rare occasion, if they were looking for someone, you might come across a random checkpoint – and that was it! Fast forward to 2020 and 2021, and by Jaysus, talk about Garda checkpoints being out in force. They were all over the shop! You couldn't go anywhere without coming across a checkpoint. I'd say the guards had a good laugh at the start listening to the absolute biggest waffle of excuses you'd ever hear, but it must have become a pain in the arse, as it went on for a lot longer than anyone could have imagined – a real stop-and-start project. Mind you, I'm sure the overtime pay was nice!

Seriously though, the Garda checkpoints became a huge part of the pandemic, especially when you couldn't go further than 5km or even 2km from your house (unless you were an essential worker of course!). No matter where you ducked or dived, there was a Garda car waiting to hear your excuse. There were roads in Ireland that people didn't even know existed until the lockdowns – not even a sheep or a mouse walked these roads before it. But sure, the Irish being Irish, we'd find some sort of way to avoid the checkpoints!

You'd often be driving on an extremely rural country road and there'd be a traffic jam, not because everyone was lined up giving yarns to the guards at a checkpoint, oh no – it was because there wasn't enough room on these bog roads for people to get by each other. You know those roads with grass in the middle, barely wide enough to get a moped down? Never mind a seven-seater SUV with all the gang heading to the beach! You had cars pulled into ditches and all with the windows down advising each other of where to go to avoid the checkpoints, and that they heard from a friend where a checkpoint might be. You'd get a good skin that would give the auld couple of flashes to warn you that there is a speed van around the corner and to slow down, and these were the same people you meet on the country roads avoiding the checkpoints to beat the band.

I had my own experience at a checkpoint one day. My head was fried, and I simply had to get to the beach for a swim. I decided I'd go to Bettystown, and I even went at six o'clock in the morning by myself, didn't bring anyone else with me. I did as much as I could to do the right thing without doing the *right* thing, if that makes sense! My plan was to get into my car, drive there, don't talk to or come close to anyone, get into the water, get back in my car and drive home. Simple as that.

Anyways, I was about halfway there, near Duleek, when I spotted a checkpoint up ahead – my God, the chances of this so early in the morning! A million things were racing through my head as I approached them. I pulled my window down.

'Well, men, how's things?'

I got a funny look off one of them. 'Where are you off to?' he says to me.

'Eh ... eh ... I'm just heading to work.'

'Where do you work?'

'Eh, Drogheda hospital.'

'And what do you do there?'

'I, eh, I wheel patients around in their wheelchairs.' (Fuck me, I had no clue what to say. I knew I hadn't the head of a doctor, so this was what popped into my head.)

'Good man, can I see your hospital badge to prove you work there?'

'Sorry, I left it in work.'

'Do you enjoy your job?'

'I do, I get great satisfaction helping the elderly.'

The other guard, who was half-listening to the conversation, looks over his shoulder and he says, 'Jaysus, ya enjoy taking the piss out of us as well, Rory, don't ya!'

I didn't know what to say. Then he says, 'So where are you really off to?!'

'Ha, sorry about that lads, I'm just going for a swim. Need it for the auld head, ya know yourselves.'

And to be fair to them, they were sound and said they enjoyed my videos (and told me to leave the poor guards alone) and said that I could go.

'Just don't make a habit of it, you know how things are at the minute!'

And off I went for my swim and thought to be myself, 'Jaysus, guards can actually be sound enough!'

## Stories from the public

*I drove from Co. Tipperary to Moate during lockdown to collect a dog that had to be rehomed.*

*I wore a nurse's uniform – sailed through all the checkpoints!*

*(Tracey B.)*

★

*Me: 'Damnit, it's the guards.'*

*Guard: 'Open your window.'*

*Me: 'I can't, I don't have a mask.'*

*Guard: 'Where do you live?'*

*Me: 'A mile up that road.'*

*Guard: 'Where are you going?'*

*Me: 'The shop.'*

*Guard: 'Show me your shopping bags.'*

*Me: Points into back seat.*

*Guard: 'OK, carry on.'*

*Me: 'Good day …'*

*How the hell could I go into a shop without a mask?*

*(Pamela S.)*

★

*I'm in the North and we live on the border. I was going down to the bottom of the hill to get diesel, which is technically across the border but two minutes from my house. A guard stops me (when the border was closed). I had my 14-year-old son in the car.*

*Guard said, 'Sorry, where are you going?'*

*I said, 'To get diesel there,' and pointed to garage.*

*He said, 'No, sorry, you're not allowed. You're going to have to turn and go somewhere else.'*

I said, 'Guard, I only live up the hill, it's the closest place.'

He said, 'No, I can't allow you.'

I said, 'Guard, I've just gotten my period and I need tampons and there is the closest place.'

He stepped back from the car, face red, and said, 'OK, go on ahead, love.'

My son was mortified. That's one way to get across.

(Leanne K.)

Driving around with boots, a halter for my horse and a bottle of penicillin on my front seat for months and telling the guards I was going to inject a sick horse at every checkpoint. Heart pounding and sweaty palms, feeling like a criminal!

(Ashling M.)

During the travel restrictions my sister and I drove around with a plate of dinner wrapped in tin foil, and if we got stopped by guards, we would tell them we were dropping our granny over some dinner.

*Our poor granny died over 30 years ago! Sorry, Granny, for lying but thanks for helping us out.*

*(Regina L.)*

*I drove over an hour and a half from where I live to collect a dog from a rescue shelter. I had my 14-year-old daughter with me, and when stopped by a Ban Garda, I told her I was dropping my daughter off at her dad's house for the weekend (I'm married).*

*On the way home, the same Garda stopped me. This time I also had a puppy barking like mad in the back of the car. I explained that her dad couldn't take her for the weekend, and he gave her the puppy as a birthday present! I said, 'Now I'm stuck with the child and the new puppy!' Her response was 'Men! Off you go.'*

*(Fiona W.)*

*Driving over to drop off my sister's birthday present with my seven-year-old daughter, I spent the whole drive telling her that if we got stopped*

*by the guards, to go along with the story that I had to drop her to her dad's for shared custody! Even took off my wedding ring! Also hung my husband's paramedic jacket over the passenger seat every time I went anywhere! Praying I wouldn't be asked to help out at an accident.*

*(Trisha C.)*

*My mam has dementia. My brother had been staying with her for a few days during lockdown and, heading back home to Cavan from Dublin, he got stopped by the guards. Asked where he was going and where he had been, he explained he had been staying with his elderly mother for a few days. Guards asked him to call her and then asked her had he been staying with her, and my poor mam – having dementia – told them she hadn't seen my brother for weeks!*

*(Deirdre C.)*

*I remember driving down to the garage outside my estate and buying a coffee, circling the estate*

*maybe 10 times blaring 'Maniac 2000' and being flagged down by guards patrolling my estate after they noticed how many times I drove past them. Had to explain I needed time away from my kids and they waved me on, thank God.*

*(Rachel C.)*

# Panic at the supermarket

Now, don't even get me started on the toilet paper and milk mini-drought. Seriously, I'd love to chat to someone who knows how and why this began. What I love about us Irish is that if we see someone else panicking, we feel that if we don't panic as well, we will be the ones left with no toilet paper to wipe our arses and no milk to put in our cornflakes. So it was an absolute domino effect, mayhem up and down the country.

Photos were going around social media of empty shelves and fridges, scaring people. I saw a couple of them myself and put down the phone straight away, got instructions from my mother not to talk

to anyone or touch anyone and get as much milk and toilet paper as I could! I even bought a few litres of skimmed milk because there was very little of that left as well. I wasn't taking any chances! I wouldn't mind, but the news and newspapers were repeatedly telling the nation that there was no shortage of products in shops and to calm the feck down, but no, the Irish were at the beginning of losing our minds. We had to leave litres of milk in the freezer and all. And as for the toilet paper, my mother still has some buried under her stairs.

## Stories from the public

*When the lockdown began, my husband rushed to Argos to get the last pasta-maker machine. He then followed this by purchasing bags of flour, and he made us all watch YouTube videos on how to make the bloody pasta in case the country runs out of food. I swear it was like he was preparing us all for a zombie apocalypse.*

*PS: The pasta machine is collecting dust.*

*(Paulina S.)*

*Eamon Ryan telling us to grow lettuce on the windowsill so we can live off it in case of food shortages.*

*(Sandra O.)*

*My son was in a queue for Dunnes back when only one person was allowed go shopping. A man and his wife ahead of him were called back by the security man and told there should be only one of them. The man, totally exasperated, at the top*

*of his voice said, 'That's my wife and I'm sleeping with her!'*

*(Anne F.)*

★

*Getting shouted at in Aldi by another customer at the cheese section for standing too close to her while she took 25 minutes to pick a cheese.*

*(Liz B.)*

# Holding in a cough and a sneeze

We were starting to hit that stage where you were so afraid of sneezing or being close to someone who sneezed in public. I remember one day being in my local Aldi. I waited my turn to go in and was walking around (this was before masks were introduced so we could still see each other), and I suppose because of the *Rory's Stories* videos some people would recognise me, so sneezing is the last bit of attention

I needed to draw on myself! Anyways, this one day I was walking around the shop, staying away from everyone, as we did, and all of a sudden, I got a woeful, and I mean woeful, itch on my nose. You see, I suffer with allergies at the best of times, so I'd be at my nose the whole time snotting and sneezing, but sneezing in public, especially indoors, during those very uncertain early Covid times was as good as holding the whole place at gunpoint.

I held in one sneeze internally and nearly felt my eyeballs pop out of their sockets with the pressure of keeping it in, not good at all for you I'd imagine, but at least I held in the sneeze and saved the whole shop evacuating with panic. But, like most sneezing fits, it didn't stop at just one sneeze, and with no major warning, I couldn't stop myself, out came a big dirty 'AHHHHCHEWWW'.

Well, I'm not joking you, if looks could kill! One woman had a bunch of apples in her hand, and she put them down, tutted at me and walked in the opposite direction. It seemed like everyone in the Aldi store had heard or seen me sneeze, and it felt like word spread that 'Your man from the videos has Covid and he's spreading it all over Aldi!' Jesus, everyone was giving me daggers. Maybe they just didn't like my comedy, I said to myself, but I'm pretty sure it was down to my sneeze!

I felt like letting out a big roar: 'I'm not riddled with Covid, I've suffered with allergies all my life, ye big paro heads, I'm grand!' But I was kind of ashamed of my sneeze, which is cracked, when you think about it. That's the way it was back in them early dark days, though. Sneezing in public was nearly a mortal sin, or it certainly felt that way, like whatever happened to a bit of dust going up your snot factory or the possibility of having a little head cold or runny nose? Nope, you sneezed in public during those uncertain days, and you had Covid, that was it, guilty as charged – absolutely bonkers, looking back at it!

## Stories from the public

*I coughed when I was on the bus and the four people in front turned around. I thought I was on The Voice.*

*(Mary R.H.)*

★

*I put my mask on straight out of my pocket but there was a piece of fluff inside it. Just walking in the door of a shop I took a breath in, the fluff got stuck in my throat and I started to cough and choke. Everyone looked at me, thinking I was riddled with Covid! I had to walk out.*

(Maggie N.)

# Covid tests

This was not an enjoyable experience. I, for one, hate anyone touching my nose. I'm always at my nose myself, like I said, sneezing and scratching it with various allergies that I have, but I don't want anyone else near it. So getting a Covid test done, or even the thought of it, for many people was harrowing! Think about it for a minute: it's an oversized ear cleaner being shoved up your nostril as far as it can go, and if that wasn't bad enough, it got twiddled around up there – you could almost feel it twiddling your eyeball!

I think everyone remembers their first Covid test experience. I got my first one done towards the end of 2020. I had a bit of a head cold and a sore throat, so as you well remember, when you had any sort of flu-like symptoms you had to get one done, and this was well before the antigen tests became available.

It was when you weren't even allowed to leave your car for your test. You rocked up to the car park, and a person appeared head to toe in spaceship attire, got you to roll down your window and asked for your details. It was so sketchy! And I had the little fella, Zach, in the back with me. He was only two at the time and he was going crazy at the head of this person coming up to our car. Little did he know that he had to get a test done too, as he had been snotting away as well the previous few days. So we didn't want to take any chances with him.

Eventually, we got the nod to drive up. I was shitting myself, because, like I said already, the thought of anyone touching my nose freaks me out. Then I see this big, long tube in her hand – it was like a skinny box of pringles, the length of it – and in that must have been the big ear cleaner, which I had to let her put up my nose and down my throat. I was starting to panic and could feel my palms getting sweaty and the sweat running down my back.

I opened the window and this lady, who seemed lovely, but felt like the reaper to me, asked me to open my mouth as far as I could. I did that, and she shoved the long bendy pencil-like thing down the back of my throat and played the drums with my tonsils. It was horrible enough, but I knew the worst was yet to come!

She then said, 'OK sir, now just tilt your head back.' I tried, but anytime she came near me I flinched, and through all this the little fella was going nuts in the back, as he thought that an alien was trying to attack his daddy.

After about five attempts I eventually built up the courage to let her at my nose, and up this stick went. The sensation is absolutely dreadful – my eyes started to piss water, and I nearly cried for my mammy to come and hold my hand! Then she said she didn't get it up far enough and needed to do it again! I thought that she was taking the piss, and I laughed at her. I thought she must have been a fan of the videos, but no, she was serious, and I had to do the ordeal again.

Once I was done another person went around the back of the car, and before Zach even knew what was going on they had it shoved up his nose. He had a delayed reaction, I think he was in shock, and then he completely lost his fucking mind, I mean roaring, and I wouldn't mind but I was only short of crying myself after this experience!

Anyways, the pair of us arrived home fairly shook after the ordeal, but thankfully on this occasion we were negative. Little did I know it wouldn't be the last time I had to get it done, but the first time is certainly the worst experience – well, for the ones who hate anyone touching their snot factory, that is!

## Stories from the public

*I remember going for my first Covid test. It was around the time the country was short on PPE gear. So I arrived with my son and was told to go to the next staff member for my PPE gear. I went over and they handed me masks and a black bag. I thought to myself, 'Jesus, things are really bad if they don't have aprons,' and proceeded to put the black bag on me, putting holes in the sides for my arms. Then I walk up to the next fella, and he says, 'Sorry, love, the bag is for your stuff like coat and mobile phone.'*

*Well, if ever there was a moment I wanted to die, that was it.*

*(Carol B.)*

*My then six-year-old was the first child to cough when they went back to school in September 2020, when they had to have a negative PCR test to go back to school. My mam posted a fiver to him for being so brave. He saw a money-making opportunity and tried to fake a cough every so often: 'Mammy, I think I need another test. Will you tell Grandma to send me a fiver?'*

*(Siobhan H.)*

# Essential vs non-essential

Now, to be a fly on the wall when they sat down to go through what was essential and what was non-essential would have been comedy gold. It was mind-blowing. It was like going into a shop and being able to buy curtains, but not a curtain rail – being told that the curtains are essential, yet the object that literally holds the curtains up is non-essential. Bizarre!

Think about it for a minute: the reason they came up with essential and non-essential was to stop congregating in shops, as in to stop people browsing and being on top of each other. Yet the off-licence part of all supermarkets was deemed essential. Don't get me wrong, I'm not complaining over that, it's a never-before-seen pandemic, we live in Ireland and if you close the drink section, blue murder would have happened. I suppose, like most, I probably relied on drink a bit too much over the lockdowns to keep me sane! But talk about not congregating! All the auld ones were recommending red wine to each other – 'Honestly that Malbec is lovely, make sure you open it early in the day to let it breathe' – in a packed off-licence aisle. All while the non-essential aisles were left free and clear!

I remember one day going into the shops to get a nail clipper, as I couldn't find one in the house and my toenails would rake the leaves off the grass. I asked a lady where they were, and she told me she thought they were in the non-essential section. I begged to differ – why wouldn't I, sure we have to cut our toenails and fingernails, don't we? Anyways, we walked down, and there was black tape over loads of stuff, including nail clippers, and what was right next door to the nail clippers in the essential part? Scissors. All the shapes and sizes of scissors you could imagine, yet the nail clippers was deemed a non-essential, like what the fuck!

The lady said, 'Sorry, nail clippers are in the non-essential section, so they are not available for purchase.' I said to her, 'What do you expect me to cut my toenails and fingernails with?' and she suggested a scissors and pointed over to a scissors that would shear a sheep. I said back to her, 'I'm not mad on how my toes look to be honest with you, never have been, but at the same time, I don't want to chop them off', and gave her a little sarcastic smirk. She gave me a stern look!

I said, 'Do the scanners not accept the barcode off the non-essential stuff, or how does it work?'

'No, it does,' says she, 'we just can't sell them.'

'Well, how about I pretend I found the nail clippers on the floor, and I brought them up to the till and you never copped it? How would that sound?!'

She looked back at me and said, 'So which size scissors would you like, sir?'

I gave in and got the smallest one and went home that evening with small, blunt scissors and made bits of my toenails!

## Stories from the public

*Elderly lady in Dunnes told me one day to lean over the barrier, pick out a dress and tell the girl at the till it was for a funeral and they would sell it to me. I did and went home delighted with my back-street dress purchase in Dunnes. I think she must have told everyone that day. There was a frenzy of people leaning over.*

*(Deirdre D.)*

*Standing outside Elverys and talking through the door to the girl inside. When she confirmed they had the Brooks Adrenaline 21 runners in stock in my size that I wanted to buy, I had to ring her to give my card details (and she still inside the door). Then she handed me out the bag. After spending €140, I walked away feeling like a criminal.*

*(Ann S.)*

*Going up to a staff member in Dunnes Stores to ask could I buy a pair of boots for work. They were literally surrounded by tape, and I could reach over and take them, but they were off-limits! So, I discreetly showed her my work badge and she told me to join the till queue and say nothing. She then took the boots, walked the long way around the tills, bagged them and whispered to the girl on the till. I nearly shat myself when I got to the top of the queue, and it was the wrong till. Next, I had to pretend I was browsing the socks beside the tills until the right till was free. She took my money and winked at me. Literally ran out of Dunnes feeling like I'd bought a kilo of drugs and sold my soul.*

*(Emma M.)*

*Decided I would go into Sports Direct for a nose around when they could open back up for 'essential workwear'. When I got to the doors I peeped in, and the place was in darkness and no music on. Suddenly, a shadow emerged from the left and asked what I was looking for. 'Ehhh, workwear,' I said, thinking that's the golden ticket in. She said,*

'That rail straight in front of you.' I walked in a bit more, and the light for that section came on. Red tape either side of this one poor shopping rail in the middle of the floor. I walked around it, trying to think of a way to get out of this. Eventually, I picked up a pair of men's work trousers, and she reappeared. 'You want those ones?' she asked. 'Em, yes please.' 'OK, straight up the stairs there, the till is on the left.' As I made my way to the stationary escalator, she got on the walkie-talkie: 'Woman on the way up there to buy trousers.' Then suddenly the escalator came on. Dead silence in the place. No music. No lights. Not another sinner around. As I ascended I looked back down at the darkness and the saleswoman staring up at me. It felt like I'd entered an episode of The Handmaid's Tale. I couldn't get out of there quick enough. Blessed be the fruit!

(Jennifer M.)

★

*In Dunnes I stepped over red tape to get to hair bobbles and the security guard started shouting at me to get out, I wasn't allowed to buy those ones, only the plain ones down by the shampoos.*

*(Jennie R.)*

*I was buying illegal red embroidery thread in Limerick. Sneaking underneath the shop barrier:*

*'Which red do you want?'*

*'That one, can I get five of 'em? I've no cash, only card.'*

*Peeking out, making sure no one was coming. Thread put in a brown paper bag and I hiding it under my coat and slipping back under the barrier like I was smuggling for Escobar himself – it was for my son's Junior Cert project!*

*(Barbara R.)*

# Getting the chop

During the lockdowns, looking after your hair was non-essential, so all barbers and hairdressers were forced to close their doors. Now, I know what you're probably thinking: *Sure, that makes no difference to you, ya have more hair on your arse than ya do on your head.* And you're correct, being bald did have its benefits during the pandemic, as I could maintain my looks with just a handy blade-one all over! But for most that wasn't the case, and people up and down the country were stressing  over their hair. Especially women. God, the thoughts of them out in the shops and the roots sticking out saying hello to everyone. 'Forget your coronavirus, what about the bleedin' state of my hair?' says she.

DIY jobs became popular but caused serious rows in households. Young lads these days love a very stylish fade, not like when I was a young fella, when we had the 'short back and sides' job. So many mothers all over the country were under pressure to not make a dog's dinner of a haircut, and some of this didn't go too well. But of course there were 'nixers' for hairdressers, and they went through the roof – the local hairdressers and barbers were hopping around the parish, sneaking in through back doors, garages and side gates to help people in bad need of a hair overhaul.

You'd be walking around the shops, and someone would be staring at your hair and go home and say, 'I saw Pauline down in Tesco's and she got her roots done. Now who would she know that would have done them for her?! She definitely didn't do them herself, too good of a job.'

Then the next time poor Pauline is out doing her shopping she'll be cornered in the fruit-and-veg aisle: 'Right Pauline, tell us, who's done your hair? I'm in bad need of getting the highlights done myself.'

Word wouldn't be long spreading, and you'd have half the town then going around proud as punch with the hair looking great. I know one local woman who got her hair done and wore a hat over it in public for about two weeks so nobody would cop she got it done. She only told me this when things were back to normal, and I was baffled. 'Why in the name of God would you bother getting it done for nobody to see it when you're out and about?' She said to me, 'Ya see, Rory, it's to feel good in yourself, don't mind anyone else.' She had a fair point!

My local barber, Paul, a gas man and long time friend, was busy hopping around a few houses doing a few cuts. If you needed a haircut, he would text saying he'd meet you in the local shop's car park and he'd park up beside you, stick his hood up, tuck his razor under his arm and make a run for your car. The minute he would get in he'd say 'Go go go' – as if he was after robbing a bank! And all the man was doing was giving a person a much-needed haircut. It's gas when you look back on it now.

The same fella was telling me a story – one day he was painting the shop (he said he'd never get a better chance to do it) and a farmer, who was over in the pharmacy across the road, spotted the car outside the shop and texted him asking, if at all possible, could he get a haircut, as it was in a very bad way. Paul agreed and told him to come into the shop. So Paul was in the shop, and he got a phone call from the farmer: 'I'm outside, is it OK to come in now?' Paul said yes, opened his door, and in ran the farmer. Paul was telling me that the farmer, who was in his mid-70s, had a hair tie in his hair that his wife had put in it to keep the hair out of his eyes. He said he had never seen such a wild head of hair in all his days; it looked like the poor man hadn't had his hair cut in over a year.

As he was cutting away at the wild head of hair, there was a tap on the door, and they heard a voice: 'Can you open up please?' Paul rushed the farmer into the back toilet and told him to be quiet.

He proceeded to open the door, and there stood two guards: 'We have been made aware that a man has come into the shop here to get a haircut …'

Paul denied this claim and said he was just doing a bit of painting to freshen up the place for when they get the nod to reopen. The guards asked for a look around and Paul agreed. So as the guards were looking around, they went into the back and said, 'Is anyone in the toilet?' and they heard a voice from the jacks saying 'No'. Paul burst out laughing and said, 'Ya can come out, Dinny.'

So out came the poor farmer, with his two hands in the air shaking and half his hair cut and the other half of his hair down to his nipples and he just looked at the guards and said, 'Before you arrest me, I was wearing a mask while my hair was being cut!' The poor fella, even the guards were giggling at this stage, according to Paul.

They agreed to let Paul finish off the haircut and warned him to keep his doors shut until further notice.

When Paul told me the story it gave me a good laugh picturing the head on the poor farmer coming out from the jacks as if he was armed with a hundred-grand-worth of cocaine!

## Stories from the public

*I remember being stopped by the Gardaí as I was going to the pet shop to get clippers for my dog, as the groomers were shut. The Garda let me go, and I passed the same Garda on the way back. He asked did I get the clippers and I said yes. I showed it to him, and he shouted to the other Gardaí, 'Lads, queue up, we're getting a haircut!'*

*(Nita C.)*

# Chapter 2: Home and Family Life

# (Hardly) working from home

Who would have ever thought you'd be working from home – or hardly working, says you! This was massive during the pandemic: all the offices cleared out, and laptops and mice sent all over the country! The number-one thing that everyone had to rely on was a solid and strong Wi-Fi connection. This was grand if you lived in a nice built-up area, but if you lived 'out in the sticks' it became a very frustrating problem.

Working from home had its pros and cons, though I can't say I know for a fact, as I wasn't working from home, but I heard and saw enough from friends to understand it. Let's look at the pros and cons:

*Pros:*

- You're starting work at 9 a.m., so you roll out of bed at 8.53 a.m.

- Wearing your PJ bottoms all day long

- Three-hour 'lunch breaks' and midday naps (don't lie!)

- No M50 traffic or being stuck on overheated, over-packed public transport
- Saving money by not paying for transport or buying lunches out on the go

*Cons:*

- Shite Wi-Fi (depending on where you live)
- Not being able to mingle or have a laugh with work colleagues
- Your living room or kitchen is your workplace from 9 to 5, so it's always there staring at you and reminding you of work!
- Thinking you're on mute when you're not (in a loud house, no less)
- Wife/husband/child making an accidental appearance during a meeting

I think everyone who worked from home has an awkward and embarrassing story to tell, some more awkward than others, whether it was thinking you are on mute and calling your boss a 'bollox' or your child repeating over your shoulder during a Zoom meeting what you said about a work colleague at the breakfast table that morning, hanging you out to dry! But at the end of the day, life moves on, and nobody cares really. As the saying goes, 'It is what it is.' So if you're embarrassed by or holding a grudge over what someone said during the pandemic over a silly Zoom call, forget about it and move on – life is too short! Just next time, make sure that the all-important mute button is on!

The PUP payment was a big help for many during the dark days. I was on it myself for a while as everything work-wise had dried up. But God, there was a fair amount of people taking the piss out of this PUP few bob! You had youngsters who were working maybe 10 hours a week in the local pub or newsagent, collecting glasses or handing out scratch cards pre-pandemic, and then all of a sudden, they were claiming it and getting 350 smackers each week! Now, don't get me wrong, do I blame them? Of course not. Would I have done it myself when I was their age? You bet your backside I would have!

In fairness to the government, it was hard to keep tabs on it. I think about 500k-plus people were out of work at one stage. It would be tough keeping tabs and means-testing that many; it was panic stations all around. It must be said it was a lifesaver for some people. That €350 was keeping food on the table in many a house around the country.

When anyone ever mentions PUP in the future, it will bring a dark memory of the pandemic back to many, but not for some teenagers who were getting the handiest €350 they would ever get. When they look back, they might think of the PUP with fond memories – the glory days of getting this lump sum each week while Mammy and Daddy were filling the fridge. Happy days for them indeed!

## Stories from the public

*My naked two-year-old son, landing in the middle of a Zoom call to give out to me for not wiping his arse, realised he was on camera and gave his bits a little wiggle for his audience.*

*(Pauline F.)*

*On a Zoom staff meeting during the first lockdown. Husband upstairs working from home and myself in the kitchen. I had three young kids bribed to watch TV and not interrupt. During the Zoom call, my two-year-old came in and I had to lift him, and everyone smiled and cooed. Then I realised he smelt awful, so I subtly texted my husband, 'Come change nappy, he has shit and it's stinking.' After a*

*few sniggers from my colleagues, I realised I had texted the work WhatsApp group.*

*(Ciara L.)*

# Home-schooling

There is one word that will forever send a shiver down every parent's spine once they hear it, and that word is 'home-schooling'. Like, how much hardship did that cause in households up and down the country during those lockdowns? When you think of it, it was hard enough to keep yourself in some sort of a positive mindset, never mind having to try teaching your children as well. For the likes of myself, who personally hated school and probably peaked in 4th class from an education point of view, this was my biggest nightmare. Admittedly, my wife did most of it while I watched *Peppa Pig* with the toddler. Talk about frying pan into the fire. But on the odd day when my wife simply had enough and couldn't do any more, I would step in, but sure what use was I in this department? I would often get headaches trying

to do some of the maths and topics that would be handed out to 3rd class pupils.

Not sure what was the point of me doing the homework with Ella, because my wife always had to check over my work – there would be full-on arguments in the house because I'd be adamant that I was correct with one or two of the questions. I won't lie, there was many a time when I would have to WhatsApp questions to my mother or my sister to find out what the correct answer was, and we're talking 3rd class work here, for *nine-year-olds,* and I'd be under pressure.

Not to mention the app Seesaw, where you had to upload your child's work onto it; that was some pain in the hole. It had a mind of its own. Sometimes it uploaded and sometimes it didn't. Listen, at the start of lockdowns, I'm sure most of us were spending the required few hours doing the home-schooling and making sure our children were learning each day, but after a couple of months of this banging-your-head-off-the-table chore, doing the odd (by odd, I mean 90 per cent of it!) bit of work yourself here and there had crept in. Sure, how could it not, burnt out with stress at this stage as we were.

There was the programme *Home School Hub* on RTÉ when the schools were shut. My *Ultimate Hell Week* buddy John Sharpson was one of the teachers on it, a sound man. Listen, like everything, it was great at the start but hard to keep the children's attention on anything for long periods, but it definitely helped a bit in the early days. It's safe to say that none of us parents wants to hear the word 'home-schooling' or see that Seesaw app ever again!

## Stories from the public

*Home-schooling the youngest, who was five at the time, and I had to send voice notes of him reading to his teacher. I was having a rough day. My 13-year-old switched the kettle on with no water in it (breaking the only thing that brought me hope every morning: coffee), and I didn't realise the voice notes were on, and the message was sent to the Junior Infants teacher, in blood-curdling screams: 'Are you f\*\*\*ing for real! I'm sick of ye all in this effin' house!' It went on for about a minute and a half of curses and screams. She just replied, 'Oh wow, sounds like there is great excitement in your house today.' Still can't look at the poor woman. Mortified.*

*(Jenna B.)*

# The Leaving Cert

When the Leaving Cert got cancelled there was nearly a celebration! I suppose there were people like me in school – the thought of sitting down at a table for two weeks writing and writing and writing would make me sweat. For all that to be whipped away from you with 'You're grand lads, no need to do the Leaving Cert this year, we'll just give you grades based on what we had seen so far in school.' Happy fecking days, says Peter from Portmarnock, who was dreading sitting the Leaving Cert but got on well with most of his teachers, just a friendly, easy-going young fella, so he has a nailed-on passed Leaving Cert in his arse pocket – nice one!

Then you had the bang of utter jealousy off the Leaving Certs of 2019, especially the ones who weren't heading anywhere near the 600-points express train, the ones who wanted that sought-after 'pass' and to head off into the big world and make something work for them! They felt a little hard done by, but sure listen, that was Covid for you – unpredictable where things were going at any time.

Who would have ever thought we would live through a time when the Leaving Cert would be cancelled? That was a big indicator that this whole thing was no joke! I for one did the Leaving Cert Applied in my school days, but I would have been doing cartwheels at the thought of the Leaving Cert being cancelled. As we Irish know, the Leaving Cert has a reputation of being the be-all and end-all! Now, I hope everyone reading this book knows it's not; yes, it's important for plenty to gauge where they are at and what course they want to do, but for plenty of others they won't get out of the Leaving Cert what their talent deserves, that's just the way the system is. Hopefully, the whole thing will change one day, and I would love to see it, because, like I've said before, we are all talented in different ways, and the Leaving Cert won't recognise some students' talents. As the old saying goes, 'If you ask a fish to climb a tree, it will spend its whole life thinking it's stupid!' That's the Leaving Cert summed up perfectly. It's a fit for some people, but not for others. Every child should be told that. Anyways, to be fair, those were very tough times for anyone who was in school, whether it was primary or secondary.

I know that school is not for everyone, but apart from getting some sort of an education, it's a place where you can go and interact with people and meet new friends. That was taken away from the youth for a good stint. And sitting at home doing school or trying to learn via a laptop? Would you stop! It's hard for loads of students to keep their attention in a classroom, never mind sitting in their bedroom looking into a screen (that hasn't got TikTok, YouTube or Instagram on it!), especially with the weather we were having during the first few months of lockdown. Very tough!

I think it may have a long-term effect on some of the youth too, unfortunately. That's why it's important that they make up for lost time. I don't really mean time in the classrooms, either, more just out playing and hanging around with each other as much as possible. There is definitely ground still to be made there. I have visited plenty of schools delivering talks, and I also did plenty over the lockdowns via Zoom. I have spoken to teachers all over the country, and they all say the same thing: that the attention spans in the classroom have dipped a fair bit since the pandemic. But sure how could it not, says you, with all the time spent away from the classrooms, and then when schools did come back first, having to wear masks? That can't be good for the head or for social skills.

It's just very important over the next few years that they work on young people's confidence and social skills again in schools, to try to get them to express themselves more and to talk and interact more with both the teachers and fellow students. Now, mind you, when I was in school, I would have been delighted at the thought of staying home from school for weeks on end, but as you get older in life you understand the importance of routine at a young age. It's vital, especially in underprivileged areas, where going to school might be someone's only source of routine. That's why we need to work with the youth as time moves on and make sure they have the confidence to fulfil their potential and not retreat into their shells too much.

My children were only aged one, three and nine then. We had our own problems keeping them entertained during the lockdowns. I'd imagine it was difficult keeping teenagers entertained and safe! Missing out on teenage discos was not ideal. Everyone can remember the craic they had at discos when they were younger, and for the guts of a year and a half, teenagers didn't get to experience them. The interaction, the dancing, the messing, the cringe chat-up lines and the sneaky can of beer pre-disco! All that was taken away from them, and that's not easy. I feel it's very important, especially in the crossroad teenage years, when you are starting to find out who you are, to be out and meeting new people and making new friends. Hopefully now, with things back to somewhat normal, the teenagers can start going out and enjoying themselves, getting up to a bit of mischief, just like we all did, because life is for living!

# Lockdown cooking

The famous feed of the lockdown was banana bread. No idea why. A bit like the toilet paper and the milk, everyone became obsessed with baking banana bread. How there wasn't a shortage of bananas in the country is beyond me. I suppose baking was something to keep the kids entertained: Rice Krispies buns, queen buns, coconut buns and banana bread.

Then you had people who would turn their living room into a restaurant at the weekends – get all dolled up, like proper dolled up, fancy dress on the lady and a tin of fruit (suit) on the man; candles lighting, lovely soft music in the background, all the best cutlery and glasses, top-class red wine and visualising being in a proper five-star hotel. I know a couple who used to do this every Friday night. They nicknamed their 'restaurant' (a.k.a. the living room)

'The Pandemic Palace'. They would put a photo of themselves up on Facebook with the caption 'Fine dining here in the five-star @ The Pandemic Palace ... Happy Friday!' It used to give me a great laugh. I suppose during those strange times it was all about having something to look forward to, and if that meant letting on you were dining out in a Michelin-starred restaurant and there was only fish, chips and beans on your plate, so be it! You were happy – well, happy as you could be, all things considered!

I also knew people who ordered dinners from fancy restaurants, and I mean *fancy*, paying loads for it, but the catch was that you had to 'assemble' the meal yourself at home. It was just like the scene in *Mrs Doubtfire* where she burns everything in the kitchen, then orders from the local five-star restaurant and has the meal looking unbelievable. So that was some people, having to heat it up and pour the sauce over it. And because they had to do this part themselves, they usually ended up burning the dinner to a crisp or eating it half-cold – it's hard to get it perfect! An auld three-in-one lathered with curry sauce would be way cheaper and less hassle!

## Stories from the public

*Passing a Chinese takeaway, I decided to go in and order, only to be told they could only take orders over the phone. So I took out my phone, stood at the desk and rang the girl who was on the other side of the desk in front of me and placed my order: the two of us, eye to eye, talking on the phone to each other.*

*(Donna O.)*

*I ordered a Chinese, go to collect it and a window opens from upstairs. A basket is lowered down by a rope, and they shout to put the money in the basket. The basket is then raised back up and the food is lowered. A quick escape to the car in case anyone sees you. So embarrassed to be that desperate for a Chinese. You couldn't make this up!*

*(Michelle P.)*

*Giving my kids burgers and chips through my bedroom window because we were pretending they were at a McDonald's drive-thru!*

*(Tara G.)*

# Songs from the shed

When we were living with my parents during the first part of 2020, myself and my father Joe decided one Saturday evening to go down to the shed and sing a song. I think it was maybe 'The Green Fields of France'. Anyways, I posted the song on social media and people really enjoyed it and asked for more! And just like that, 'A Song from the Shed' was born and every Saturday night we would go down to the shed and sing an Irish classic.

We sang 'Grace', 'Nancy Spain', 'Rare Auld Times' and 'Raglan Road' to name a few. It was good craic and people seemed to enjoy the song each week. It was a real lockdown thing to do but it gave ourselves and others a little taste of being in the pub and that sing-song atmosphere we all craved during those days!

# *Normal People* and abnormal TV

Some of the stuff that was on live TV in Ireland during the lockdowns was comical. A few things stick out in my mind: remember they did the *Claire Byrne Live* show from her shed? Like, who would have ever believed that? That's how terrified everyone was of the virus. And on one of her shows they discussed what a live event might look like in the future, and you had two people in these big plastic bouncing balls. Classic stuff! We had officially lost the plot!

Then you had *The Late Late Show* showing people how to do home haircuts. And most of the politicians were too afraid to cut their own hair, as the public might think they got a barber to do it. God, Simon Harris sticks out in my head when I think of people who badly needed a visit to the barber's. Poor fella had hair coming from all angles!

One of the massive TV hits of the pandemic was *Normal People*; it kind of gripped the nation. I watched it as well. It was very good. It aired when myself and my family were living with my parents, and one of the evenings, we all (my parents and my wife) decided after dinner to watch the latest episode, as we had missed out on it in real time (God bless modern TV). Such an episode to miss out on, it was one of them that was pretty much 'all action', if you get me. Jesus Christ, even though I'm in my mid-thirties, it was still so awkward watching it with my parents sitting five feet away from me on the other couch. No matter how old you get, shite like that is never anything but awkward. At one stage during one of the full-on scenes, my wife texted me saying, 'Ground, swallow me up quick', and my auld lad, being a messer, says, 'Now, you lovebirds, don't be getting any ideas by this stuff.' I laughed, but my wife nearly died!

In all honesty, it was a great series, great storyline to it! Paul Mescal became a cult hero after it, from playing minor football with Kildare to making white O'Neills shorts famous around the world. I think even Gucci brought out their own style of GAA shorts. Either way, it was a great hit, and a good watch during lockdown, albeit a much better and less awkward watch without your parents in the same room as you!

# The TikTok phenomenon

Was there a house in Ireland that didn't make a TikTok during the lockdowns? No matter what age you were, you stuck your noggin on the social media app at some stage.

It really blew up during the pandemic. I think the song every household shook their hips to most was 'Laxed (Siren beat)' (I did anyway – and the cut of me!). I don't have a TikTok account myself, I'll leave that to the younger generation! My daughter Ella has a private account, and we did the odd one on that. It was the perfect platform for everyone to make an eejit out of themselves for a laugh and a giggle. At that time, we had a lot more to be worried about, so letting loose on TikTok was nothing to worry about or stress about, and it often kept the boredom at bay!

# Online shopping sprees

If there was one thing that blew up during the pandemic it was online shopping. It had become more and more popular over the past few years, but during the lockdowns, it went to another level! I know in my own house it went through the roof. Most days I would be answering the door to a DHL driver – he was the one person I had seen most outside of my family during the pandemic! Ding-dong would go the doorbell, and he'd be there – 'Package for Emma' – and off he would go.

How do you know when you have a problem with online shopping? I'll tell you how:

- You freak out when stuff leaves your 'basket', like proper freak out!

- You order stuff online knowing well you won't be wearing it.

- ❋ You ask the delivery driver to knock next door and leave the package there if your partner's car is in the driveway.

- ❋ You know the delivery driver by their first name.

- ❋ You have added them as a friend on Facebook, and if a delivery you had expected to come on a certain day didn't arrive, you message him: 'Hi Slav, I hope all is well with you and your family, you are doing a great job. Keep up the good work during these uncertain times. Mind yourself and all the best, Paula (number 123 Main Street, the one with the red door)'. What you really mean is, 'Where is my top that I ordered from ASOS, the one that I probably won't ever wear and will send back, but that doesn't matter, I was expecting my doorbell to ring today and it didn't, where the feck are ya?!'

That's when you know you have a problem. But one thing I will say is, you're not alone!

## Stories from the public

*I remember going into Dunnes to get the little one shoes and bringing them to the till, and the girl's like, 'You can't buy them.'*

*Me: 'Why?'*

*Her: 'Covid restrictions, sorry. But you can order them for click and collect.'*

*Me: 'Where do I collect them from?'*

*Her: 'Just order online and then come in here and collect them at the till.'*

*(Aoife E.)*

# Staycations

'Staycation' was a popular word during the pandemic. Once things started to open up, we couldn't really leave the country, so everyone was excited booking up everywhere in Ireland, from Kerry to Donegal. All the hotels were booked up – and booked up fast! Even the not-so-popular spots, we'll say, were booked out, and the *prices* – let's not get into that!

Then you had to book a time for breakfast, book a time for dinner, book a time for swimming, nearly had to book a time for brushing your teeth. Pure hardship!

We went on our own little staycation to Cork. Now, anyone reading this book who has young children will appreciate the effort it takes to even get on the road, never mind getting to the destination. The packing that goes on when you have a gang, holy God, give me strength – especially when you have a couple of nippers under the age of three! A billion nappies shoved in a bag, the boot absolutely wedged, and the bag of 'distracters' (nibbles, juices, crisps, fruit, rattlers, phones, iPads, books, toys … whatever will keep them from screaming!) sorted, then away ya go.

During the whole car journey to your destination, you will say the below, again and again and again:

- 'I'm warning you, if you don't stop fighting, I am turning this car around and we are going home.'

- 'How are you hungry again? We only just stopped in a garage!'

🦠 'Let her watch the iPad for a few minutes to keep her quiet.'

🦠 'It's not my fault there's no coverage on these roads, play 'I Spy' there, like I had to when I was your age.'

🦠 'Did you fart?! No? Must be the baby again. Feck's sake, we need to pull over to change her.'

🦠 'I tell ya, you'd really notice the price of fuel when you go on these long drives!'

🦠 'Listen, we will be there when we are there!'

Then you had to depend on the good aul Irish weather to make or break your staycation. One thing in this world you can rely on is that you can't rely on Irish weather! No matter if it's smack-bang in the middle of the summer, there will always be a 'chance of rain' in this country, and when you have this perfect little family holiday planned in your mind – in and out of the sea, the kids building sandcastles, eating 99s, putting sun lotion on yourself to try to get a nice tan, even popping in the earphones, closing your eyes and letting yourself imagine you are in Spain – there is a good chance you'll be stuck indoors, looking out at the rain while the kids drive you up the walls! Staycations are a nice option to have, don't get me wrong, I love this country, but give me Portugal or Spain any day of the week for a family holiday!

# Lockdown Lucy

When my family and I were living with my parents in 2020, Emma became pregnant with our third child, Lucy. We had always wanted and planned for three children, but we didn't exactly plan to be living under my parents' roof, and in the middle of a pandemic, when it did happen. But sure that's life, you never know what's around the corner!

You're probably wondering how it even happened in the first place, living under my parents' roof and no hotels open to get away for a night! Anyone who has had to move back into their parents' house to save for a mortgage will understand the craic there.

For my generation (I was born in the late 1980s), the issue is the price of rent and houses. You're sometimes left with no choice but to move back in with the parents to try to save the deposit to buy a house. For most people, renting a house while trying to save for a mortgage just isn't possible in this day and age.

Anyways, on a very rare occasion, we might 'chance it'! So, with the kids settled in bed, we would go upstairs earlyish of a Friday night and see if we could get away with it.

Well, one night I told Emma to head on up to bed and I'd go into my parents and somehow try to throw some sort of a hint without making things dreadfully uncomfortable and awkward for us. I popped the head into the backroom; *The Late Late Show* had just started. I said, 'Right so, myself and Emma are heading up to bed to get an early night. Is that fair enough?' That's no bother, they said. I made sure to look my father straight in the eye as if to say, 'You know the craic now, don't ya? I don't need to explain this to you – don't dream of coming up the stairs for at least half an hour!'

I closed the door and ran up the stairs to brush the teeth, almost re-enacting Colm Meaney in the Roddy Doyle film *The Snapper*! I jumped into the hay, and I'd say my boxers hadn't even hit my ankles when I heard the hall door opening and a big unit pounding up the stairs! Panic stations in the bedroom.

'Don't tell me that's my da coming up the stairs. Is he for fucking real?'

Like a bull, I sat up and told Emma I was going in to say something. She pleaded with me not to, as it would have been too embarrassing, but I didn't listen to her. Slung my T-shirt on and made a dart for my parents' bedroom, which isn't exactly in the 'east wing' – it's about 12 feet from the bedroom we were staying in. The door was closed, and the dad had the bedside lamp on. Out of respect, I knocked on the door before arrival, then closed the door behind me so neither Emma nor my mam could hear the conversation.

'Da, what ya playing at?'

'Ah, your mother is watching *The Late Late* and I've enough of it, so just going to read a book here. Everything OK?'

'Is everything OK, he says,' I half muttered to myself. 'Da, c'mon, surely ya know the craic, like in all honesty, will ya give me a break here?!'

The penny dropped with him then, 'Oh Jesus, I'm sorry, I didn't cop on what was happening.'

'Well, Da, to be fair, we are married and don't have our own house and the kids are in bed and it's Friday night. Ya don't need a calculator to figure it out, do ya?!'

'No, Jesus, no, I'm sorry. I'll put the clothes back on and head downstairs for a bit, give you lovebirds some peace!'

'Nah, ya can't do that, because Emma will know that I said something, and the door will be shut for more than just tonight! Listen, in future have a bit of cop-on, will ya? Put yourself in my shoes and imagine the hassle this is for us. Do ya get me?!'

'One hundred per cent, bud. Next time, you just give me the nod and I won't budge!'

I closed the door, took a deep breath and went back into our bedroom, while all along tippy-toeing so I didn't wake up the toddler – the carnage would be real! When I got back into our bed, I had no choice but to count sheep and try to fall asleep. You see, that's the joys of having to move back in with your parents. No matter what age you are, the job you have, whether you're married, have kids, it doesn't matter, once you're under their roof you still feel like you are 14 years old again!

I remember going to the fridge to get out cans of beer during the early lockdown days, when drinking five cans a night was nearly normal, and the eyeballing I'd get from the mother with each can I took!

'Ah Rory, are ya drinking again? You're getting too fond of that stuff.'

*Take a deep breath, Rory, and try not to flip!* 'Mother, *please*, I'm not 15 anymore. The world has gone to fuck, I'm not sure if I'll even have work again. I don't have a house and I've two kids upstairs, a wife stressed off her head about the future and here you are giving me hassle over a few cans. Please, I beg ya, please!'

But even with very little opportunity to have some 'us time', Emma did manage to fall pregnant with our third child. We felt like we were teenagers again, afraid to tell my parents, because with the world all over the shop at that time it was unclear if we would have our own house anytime soon! But sure listen, you just have to remain positive. So we made sure we had solid tactics for when the best time would be to tell my parents the news that Emma was expecting a baby in December. Like most Irish households, we waited for a Friday night, when everyone was having a few drinks and was merry. We said it after the dinner, and thankfully it was positive vibes all around. To be fair to my parents, we were already in the house with two kids and just about squeezing in, and another would have been hectic, but I made the pledge to my parents that, by hook or by crook, we would have our own place once the baby arrived. If we had to go back to paying mad money for rent, so be it, but our own home would be magic. We thankfully worked with a good broker at McCarney Financial Services. I would have known Ciaran previous to this, as he was a selector for my club's senior team in the past, and I would have played football with his son Jack. A sound man is Ciaran, a very educated and smart man from Finglas, the perfect blend of knowledge and street smarts!

He and his daughter Aisling went above and beyond for us and finally landed us with our mortgage. I have to say, and anyone who has been lucky enough to be in a position to be told their mortgage has been approved will understand, that it really is a special feeling – a weight lifted off your shoulders. I remember being in my parents' kitchen the morning Ciaran rang us with the good news. Emma started crying straight away, and I wasn't far from it myself, to be honest! It was just such a relief that we could now go and try to find somewhere for us to live.

We looked around and found a place in Ashbourne that we felt was ideal, and we moved into our new home in August 2020. To this day, we are very grateful to have a roof over our heads, and I never wanted to live anywhere other than my home town, Ashbourne, so to have that is certainly a dream come true. The neighbours are lovely as well, loads of Dubs, so plenty of slagging on the road over football, but really down-to-earth people, and that's what makes a good housing estate!

# The snip

As I said, Emma and I had always wanted three kids, and we are very thankful to be blessed with Ella, Zach and Lucy. So after surviving lockdown with a nine-year-old, a very wild toddler and a baby, myself and Emma decided I needed to get the 'snip' done. Every man's worst nightmare! But we both decided it was the right thing to do, as we were very happy with the three kids, and wanted to move forward in life, get away from nappies, tantrums and soother runs! Getting our life back at 40 is the plan!

It's not an easy thing for a man to commit to, but after a lot of inner conversations, I plucked up the courage and made the phone call. When a lady answered the phone I said, 'How's things, I'm looking to get the job done on myself, unfortunately. Would you have any appointments?'

'OK, it's a vasectomy you're looking for?'

'No, no, the snip, ya know the one that stops ya having more babies.'

She chuckled and said, 'Yes, that's called a vasectomy.'

'Oh God, I'm sorry. Yeah, one of those please.'

You have to go in for a pre-consultation before your actual appointment, and any man will tell you that this is a very strange conversation. Even though it's just two adults having a chat, I felt like a 10-year-old sitting there! Anyways, after going through in detail what the operation consisted of, I officially booked an appointment to get the job done.

I was absolutely shitting myself, for obvious reasons, and when I turned to the wife for some sympathy the morning of the 'big operation' (or 'little procedure', as she called it), she told me to stop crying like a little boy and reminded me that she had gone through labour – three times!

So off I went, cold sweat running down my forehead, and arrived at the clinic.

'Well folks, I'm here to get the job done.'

I was brought into a room. Three women followed me in, and one told me, in as nice a way as possible, to 'Lie down on the bed there and pull your boxers down below your knees.' I did what I was told and started to realise that this was happening. 'Oh my God, what am I doing here?' rang around my head.

'Sir, you are going to feel a little pinch, as we are going to inject some local anaesthetic into your testicles.'

I didn't know where to look or what to say. I was kind of in shock at what was about to happen, so I just moved my toes in approval.

As one of the ladies was working away on my golden jewels, the other lady says, 'So, Rory, have you any shows coming up?'

I thought to myself, '*Oh my Jaysus Christ* ... they know who I am!' Like honestly, can you imagine anything more awkward than that?

I stuttered and farted and then said, 'Ehh, yeah, yeah, coming back soon, thank God, be great to get back on stage again, ya know?!'

And just like that, the other lady, who was making hay on my – let's just say groin area – perks up and says, 'Ah Rory, my husband loves your work. We both get a great laugh out of your videos. You kept us going during lockdown.'

Now, all this is going on while my boxers are around my ankles, more exposed than I had ever been in my life!

I nearly fainted with embarrassment, so I started to count to 10 over and over in my head until the procedure was done.

Fifteen minutes later, after I got the nod that the job was done, I pulled up my boxers, failed to make eye contact with the lovely ladies and left the room, walking like John Wayne on a bad day.

I had a glass of water in the waiting room to digest what had just happened, and eventually left and drove home with a soft pillow under my arse, protecting myself from any ramps or speed bumps on the way home.

Sure listen, it's not ideal and is certainly not on any man's bucket list, but I believe the procedure has been very popular since lockdown, as people had too much time on their hands! So I'm not the only man with his jocks around his ankles in front of strangers these days. Thank God!

# Chapter 3: Social Life (Or Lack Thereof)

# Small talk

In Covid times, when you stopped to talk to people on your daily walk it was a nightmare trying to find things to talk about. Pretty much every conversation across the country was the same:

'Well, how's things, any news?'

'Nah, nothing. You?'

'Nah, sure same old. Mad, isn't it?'

'I know yea, mad!'

'Numbers are very bad, aren't they?'

'Yeah, terrible.'

'It's nice though, to slow down for a while, isn't it? Ya know, bit of family time.'

'Yeah, defo.'

'God, we'll appreciate the normal times when they come back, still, won't we?'

'Yeah, that's for sure.'

(Bit of an awkward silence for a few seconds, both people wanting to delay their walk, but both with absolutely nothing to talk about)

'Anyways. Yeah, it's just mad!'

'I know, mad.'

'Right. I might go. I'm sure I'll see ya tomorrow no doubt.'

(A real sarcastic laugh)

'Ha, yeah, no doubt. G'wan, stay safe!'

And off you'd go. It was so weird, the Irish way of saying goodbye to each other after a chat was always, 'Right, g'wan, mind yourself, bye-bye,' etc. But for these strange times, everyone finished their goodbyes with a 'stay safe'.

It's funny how the conversations and outlooks would change as time went by, too. The first three weeks was, 'The bit of downtime is what's needed in this world. Everything was just moving too fast. We needed this reset button to appreciate the simple things in life.'

And then, in the next three weeks it was, 'We all have to do our best. We need to stay at home and protect the vulnerable. We are in this together.'

But six months later it turned to, 'Do ya know what? I'm so fucking sick of it at this stage. It's doing my head in. I just don't see any end to this. Nobody seems to have a clue what they're doing.'

# Bottle-bank banter

Bottle banks in the country were never as busy as during the pandemic. Especially during the first lockdown, when the weather was top class, plenty of bottles of beer and wine were sank under the blue skies. Everyone was stuck out in their back gardens with nowhere to go, and the smell of BBQ in the air every evening was great. We were blessed with the weather we got – that must have been said a thousand times up and down the country during March, April and May 2020:

'If it wasn't for the weather, I don't know what we would do.'

'Have ya ever seen weather like this? God, without it we'd be lost.'

'Isn't the weather we're having just a miracle? All the sadness around us, but the clear skies are helping for sure. Up Ireland, up sunshine!'

You know as well as I do how much we Irish hope and pray for the weather being good. Either way, we'll talk about it, but for those few months of early lockdowns, it surely was a blessing. And the hot temperatures led to very thirsty mouths, so off-licences were busier than ever, as was every bottle bank the length and breadth of the country.

People had different tactics with the bottle-bank runs. Some would go every week and clear out what they had, and others might go every month, but there was an awkwardness when you saw people at the bottle banks and you would have more empty bottles in your boot than you would find at Electric Picnic!

'Ah good man, Rory, how's the form?' would be said to me as I rocked up with a wheelbarrow spilling over with empty bottles.

'Not too bad.'

'Ya look like you're enjoying the auld lockdowns!'

'Ah, Jaysus no, I might have the odd bottle at the weekend. All these are from last Christmas. I was just clearing out the shed.'

'Ha, yeah, I'd say that alright.'

'No, honestly, and I actually knocked into a couple of neighbours to see if they wanted me to bring down any of their empties – ya know, save them the hassle!'

Jesus, some people are gone mad on this Covid. I knocked into my neighbour asking if she wanted me to bring any down and bejaysus she lit on me for touching her door, roared down at me from the top bedroom window. She threw three bottles of gin at me, so she did.'

'I hope they were full,' says he.

'Ha, I wish they had been full. Not a drip in them, so that's why I have so many empty bottles. Ya probably won't see me here again now till next Christmas.'

After an episode like that, you have to have a tactical plan for when you're gonna show your face again at the local bottle bank, either very early in the morning or very late at night – that's your only hope of not looking like a right pisshead, which a lot of us were, to be fair!

Another way of looking at it is that we Irish have major issues with what people think of us. It's nearly like tradition at this stage: 'What will the neighbours say?' It's personally something I would just love to see stop. In this day and age, who cares? There is so much madness going on in the world, we need to be free like birds and stop caring what other people think of us. It's the only way you'll be on the road to happiness, in my opinion, and being ashamed of going to the bottle bank too often in the middle of a pandemic sums that up! Be yourself, be sound, be happy!

# A cocktail for disaster

No point in denying the fact that home drinking went through the roof during the lockdowns. One popular activity in many a house of a Friday night (or midweek, depending on how bad a day you were having!) was making home-made cocktails. Now, I'll be honest, I am not a cocktail man at all. I'm one of them that had bad experiences over the years with them, and no more so than on my honeymoon!

We had gone to Cancún and stayed in an all-inclusive place. After a few days, I was sick of the local beer, so I said I would give a few cocktails a go. Well, what a mistake that was! Even writing this and bringing my mind back to that night is making me feel sick. I must have had about ten, and was absolutely goosed, full to the boot on cocktails. At the time I thought they were the nicest things ever. Having the time of my life I was, telling everyone in the bar to settle down and be quiet and listen to me butcher 'Grace' after giving an Irish history lesson to these Americans, Dutch and French strangers, who must have thought I was cracked. They weren't wrong, says you!

Anyways, I got back to the room at bonkers o'clock, and shortly after that, the puking began! I must have been down on my knees having a conversation with the toilet bowl for a good three hours – it was horrific! The killer was the grapefruit in a few of them, and I belched grapefruit for the next two days. If I even smell grapefruit now, I'll heave right there and then! Everyone has a certain food or drink that they have had a bad experience with. Well, that's me and grapefruit – done for life, we are!

I'd be lying if I said I had too many cocktails during the lockdowns, but I know plenty of you had your cocktail parties, invested in elaborate cocktail kits during the early stages of lockdown and challenged yourselves to make new cocktails every week for your virtual drinks party (virtual chaos is what I mean!).

My wife has a friend who made home-made margaritas for New Year's Eve 2020 and spilled margaritas all over her work laptop. Not ideal! She can still smell alcohol off it to this day. She'll always remember that New Year's Eve – the sticky keys will make sure she never forgets!

## Stories from the public

*Having my dad's birthday get-together in my back garden and getting him and my brother priest costumes, as back then you could meet for Mass, so the deal was if the guards called to the door, we were having a family Mass.*

(Sharon W.)

# The perfect pint

When pubs were closed, cans of porter became a thing. There were so many different rumours and tips going around for how to make the perfect-tasting pint out of a can. Does such a thing exist? Definitely not! But we all gave our various tactics a rattle during the dark days, such as the following:

- Freeze the glass before pouring your can in.

- Pour the first two-thirds of your can in first, then wait five minutes and pour in the rest, just like they do with your pint in the pub.

- Throw the can straight in, let the stout come up around the rim of the can and then pull the can out of the glass slowly.

- Pour the can into the glass while banging the can off the sides of the pint glass on the way up.

- Drink the pint in no more than three sups, as this will keep the 'shtick' around the glass, which usually means a better pint.

Truth be told, it was just porter in a can, and no matter what we did to make it better, it was still a scuttery pint that we had convinced ourselves was nice. Now, towards the latter end of the pandemic, Guinness brought out the Nitrosurge cans, which was defo a bit of a game-changer. Don't ask me how, but I bought one myself, and have to say the pint is better tasting and there's more shtick to the can. Another positive of these surge cans is they have a couple more millilitres of stout in them, which means your pint fills right up to the top. The original Guinness cans stopping just short of the rim of the pint glass was a real pet hate of mine. Anyways, it's fair to say that nothing will ever beat a creamy pint in a cosy pub, but for the lockdowns, the cans of porter served us well, and it proved to be a bit of craic trying out various ways to pour the best pint from a can. All hail pubs being back open!

# Dining out

Outdoor dining became the big thing during the pandemic as it was understood that you are less likely to catch Covid outdoors. This was all fun and games while the weather was lovely, bright and sunny, and bar and restaurant owners were finding any space at all to throw out a few tables and chairs and bring in a bit of custom, and sure, weren't they dead right?

One big issue with this was there was nowhere to go to the toilet, as you weren't allowed indoors.

# Social Life (Or Lack Thereof)

*I'll serve ya 10 pints of stout no bother, but ya may hold it in till ya get home!* Not possible, so the 'keep sketch' was back alive and well: one of your friends would go and clear the bladder while the others kept an eye out. Sure, what else were you meant to do? As bad as this was for men, I can only imagine the hassle it was for women, as it's handy enough for a male to find a little spot to drain the spuds, but it's more of an ordeal for women. Especially if you have had a few too many on you and you're trying to squat down, all your Joe Wicks home workout classes were put into practice to ensure you had a strong-enough squat stance to do the business safely and successfully. But if you either fell backwards on your arse or forward on your head you weren't the only one, I'd imagine! Thank God for pub toilets, says you. They won't be taken for granted again!

And then you had dining and drinking outdoors during the winter. Now that was diehard stuff. Sitting out in a smoking area in Ireland, during the winter, under a heater and having an overpriced pint while chatting to your mates – was this appealing? It actually kind of was, considering the really bleak days, but it certainly wasn't what you would like to call 'normal'! If you were lucky enough to get under a heater, it was grand ... for a while, until it became hotter than the Sahara under it. The only other option was to enjoy your drink with five layers on you, while your hand was shaking trying to get the gin and tonic up to and into your mouth successfully! Then you had a race against time. In the early days, you only had an hour and a half at your sitting before you were booted out for the next crew to arrive: 'How's things, don't mind the food, we'll have the cheapest thing on the menu – just bring a bottle of champagne. Everyone, six minutes until our time is up or one of us passes out ...'

You had people necking their drink as they were being escorted out of the building: 'How the hell is that 105 minutes already? Sure, I was only starting to rant to my friends about how much my husband and kids wreck my head!'

Not to mention when you were only allowed a maximum of six people at a table, so if your 'lifelong friends' group had eight people in it, two of them had to get the short straw and sit away from everyone else. They could only keep up with the chats and the gossip via the WhatsApp group as they sat over the other side of the restaurant. Bleak indeed. Normality in a restaurant and pub environment was never more welcome!

## Stories from the public

*Last summer, when the pubs were only serving outdoors, I arranged to meet a friend in the beer garden of a local pub. In she comes with her own empty pint glass from home and asked the barman to fill her beer into that. By the time she was ordering her fifth, she didn't care if he filled the pint into her shoe.*

*(Mary O.)*

*Having a drink in my local, it was gone past the curfew and the owner spotted the guards in his camera. The few left ran up to the back area like a herd of cattle in fear. All hiding in the toilet afraid to take a breath. Guard knocking on the door. Someone farted and we nearly passed out with the smell. The sweat was pouring off me, thinking, 'What will the neighbours say if I'm caught after eight in the pub?' Texted my 19-year-old son to be ready to do a drive-by the minute the guard moved. Longest 10 minutes of my life; nearly lost a stone weight with the stress. The guard eventually left and the few of us tiptoed out and ran off in*

*different directions. I hopped into my son's car like I was after doing the great robbery, and then hiding in the back seat with fear.*

*(Carmel K.)*

★

*Going into a pub to get a bit of bar food and not a sinner in it:*

*Barman: 'Eh, sorry, have ya booked a table?'*

*We're standing there looking at him, place completely empty.*

*Me: 'No, sorry, we haven't. Can ya fit us in there?'*

*Barman: 'No, sorry, you have to ring us to book a table.'*

*Me: 'So if I go outside the door and ring you, we can have a table?'*

*Barman: 'Yes.'*

*He was doing his job I know, but we did laugh.*

*(Janet O.)*

# Bags of cans and takeaway pints

Who doesn't love a 'big bag of cans'? I would have grown up well used to the big bag of cans and off to a field with yourself. It was a great night out. Now, we didn't do this by choice but because we were too young to go to any pub, this was our only option! Well, who would have thought in the year 2020 it would be your only option again? I'm 35 years old and mad for a session with my mates, so a bag of cans and an open field it was. At least this time around I could go into the shop and buy my own cans, and didn't have to wait by the side of the shops for ages seeing if someone would go in and get them for me!

In fairness, though, when you're hiding around a corner and you see this 'adult' coming out of the shop with a big bag of lovely cans (even if they were pissy Dutch Gold), what a feeling that was, up there with Christmas morning as a six-year-old!

Then you had the takeaway pints and the pubs that started delivering pints to your door. Ingenious! A little knock on the door, you'd open it with excitement and there would be four creamy pints of stout staring at you. Sheer happiness after you've been drinking cans of Guinness for the past few weeks.

The government then brought in a rule about only being able to drink your takeaway pint 100m from the pub, so there would be large groups of people gathering around the corner from the pub, completely defeating the point. It wasn't the first time a restriction made absolutely no sense, but sure listen, everything was all over the shop. A bag of cans with your friends on a mild 2020 evening, digesting what was happening in the world won't be forgotten, though. It was therapy at the time is what it was!

## Stories from the public

*A few months in, after the start of the first lockdown, a few of us said we would go up the railroad tracks for a couple of cans and a chat since we hadn't met in ages, and we hadn't done it since being teens with flagons and naggins. So we were up under the tracks in the middle of nowhere and slightly pissed, and one of the lads said, 'Imagine if the guards came up this lane.' Thirty seconds later, two guards with high-vis on came around the corner and found eight nearly-50-year-olds in the middle of nowhere who couldn't answer any of their questions from roaring laughing. They walked off laughing and left us alone. They thought it was kids they were coming for.*

*(Colm C.)*

# The €9 rule

If all this wasn't mad enough, then some genius came up with the idea that if you buy a meal worth €9 with your drink you have less chance of picking up the virus. To this day I can't get my head around that theory. It was very unfair for pubs that didn't have any kitchen facility, although from what I heard it didn't stop some of them. Sure, I know one pub, what they did was they had a burger van across the road on Friday, Saturday and Sunday. A burger and chips were €10, and you got a ticket for a pint when you went out and got this meal deal.

Sure, everyone was winning. If you didn't fancy a pint there was a nice burger van in your location, and if you did fancy a pint, you could just have your burger and chips at whatever time you wanted and have your few pints later. Mad that pubs had to do all this to make some sort of business for themselves after being under severe pressure for the guts of a year. You'd walk into so many pubs across the country, and you would see loads of baskets of chicken and chips and half-eaten pizzas and burgers lying everywhere. Ridiculous!

The problem with all this craic was that common sense was not very common at all, and I'll give you a perfect example. I remember when this €9 meal with your drink thing was in full flow, and I was staying down the country in a hotel with the family. I went out to visit my relations, had a BBQ and a few drinks with them, and my wife drove as she was pregnant at the time. When we got back to the hotel it was about 8.30, and I fancied a nightcap. So Emma went on up to the room with the little man, and myself and Ella went into the bar. I asked if I could have a pint, please, as I was a resident, and the lady said I'd have to eat something worth €9 before she could serve me a pint! I went on to say that I wasn't hungry and that I just had a BBQ, but I would love a pint if that's OK!

She explained to me that the rules are the rules and that I need to order food worth €9, resident or no resident, though to be fair she said it in as nice a way as possible! I said, 'Fair enough, so' and looked at the menu. The starter portion of wings was €7, and I saw garlic bread was €4, so I said I'd get the wings for myself and the garlic bread for Ella, even though neither of us was hungry. So when the lady came back to take our order, she asked me if both were for me and I said no, my daughter was having the garlic bread and I'd be having the wings.

She then said, 'I'm so sorry, but one person has to order €9 worth of food, not between them!' I looked at her, half laughing, thinking, 'Am I being punked here? Does she follow my stuff online and wants to have a bit of craic with me?' But no, she had a fairly stern look on her face when I laughed, and she said, 'Well, are you ordering?'

I said, 'OK, so I'll have the garlic bread *and* wings, and Ella here will have garlic bread as well.' She took the order and off she went. I sat there thinking to myself: 'Is this it? Is this what normality is going to be like? If so, then we're in big trouble!' Thankfully the rules were scrapped, but I suppose it still proves that, like I said, common sense is not really that common … especially during a pandemic!

Talk about a waste of food! The world was in a dire place, with Covid of course but also with loads of starving people around the world. Yet you come to Ireland and there was food wasted left, right and centre in every pub across the island! Honest to God, only in this country would that happen or would a rule like that be brought in!

If you walked into a pub you could tell by looking at the leftovers who had been on the beer all day. You'd have a couple sitting there with gin and tonic glasses lined up and a head of a man with 12 pints of stout on him, and in front of them would be four carvery dinners, with the odd chip touched and the rest sitting there stone cold. Madness, when you think back at it. Soakage defo wasn't a problem in them days!

## Stories from the public

*While in a restaurant with my mother, I ordered a large fish chowder and my mam ordered a small fish chowder. We go to order drinks and the waitress says to me, 'You can have a drink, but she can't,' and points at my mother. Why? Because my soup cost over €9 and my mother's didn't. Some holiday that was!*

*(Fiona B.)*

# Takeaway coffee vans

Coffee was defo already popular in Ireland pre-pandemic. I had even jumped on the bandwagon myself, having never had a cup of coffee until 2010 when I went to Australia, where I chanced a 'flat white' with my brother-in-law Bren, and from that moment I became a 'coffee head'. It's only in the past few years that it really took off in Ireland, and the coffee craze went especially mad during the pandemic.

The takeaway coffee vans became a huge hit. They were popping up everywhere, and not only could ya get your coffee in all shapes and sizes, but the toasties became a huge hit as well. Mind you, you'd pay dearly for your toastie, but they were class the few that I had.

It's kind of sad, but going for a coffee and a stroll was lots of people's highlight of the day during the lockdowns. It was nearly the one thing keeping people half sane. They'd be saying to themselves, 'Right, I'm getting out of this house at 11 a.m. to meet Linda for a coffee and burn the ears off her, so just get to 11 a.m. C'mon, you got this!' As they were looking at their child drawing on the walls with a permanent marker!

You had people who had only ever had a Maxwell House coffee once in a blue moon pre-pandemic suddenly become a coffee expert, all, 'Can I have a vanilla latte with skimmed milk, please?' You knew it was a tough day when you land down at the coffee van for the third time that day, stressed off your head: 'Can I just have an espresso please, and if you put an extra shot into it, I won't mind tapping my card for it!' People were going around caffeinated to the eyeballs.

To be fair, it's not just in the pandemic that the coffee was needed to survive! To this day, I need coffee to get through the day. I think anyone who has young kids will relate to that. When you have had a shitty night with them, in and out of their rooms a dozen times during the night, soother runs, etc., coffee is a lifesaver the following morning, mid-morning, lunchtime, mid-afternoon and even that evening some days! Anything to get you through the day when you have young nippers!

# Zoom, Zoom, Zoom

Can any of us truly say we ever heard of Zoom before this whole pandemic came about? The Zoom quizzes that everyone got stuck into, especially during the first lockdown, like, in all honesty, how painful were they? Having a few drinks on a Friday evening, getting excited to sit in front of your laptop and play a quiz with your friends – that's proper pandemic madness right there. I'd say the first one for most people was kind of exciting, as it was something different, and was a chance to remember what your friends looked like! But Jaysus, after two or three of them they became fairly boring.

There were always different characters on these Zoom quizzes, you had:

**The Interrupter.** This person would just not shut up and let anyone else speak. They kept butting in all the time, and the more they drank the more listening to them rabbit on would become a torture, and most often quizzes would finish earlier than expected because this dose was wrecking everyone's head!

**The Dry Arse.** You know well that this person had absolutely no interest in getting involved in any sort of craic or banter. They were there yawning into the laptop two minutes after logging in, supping away on their weak tea and nibbling on their dry digestive biscuit, bringing zero buzz to an event where it was already hard enough to get the craic going. It's not just the

pandemic that had brought out the boredom in this person, they'd been like that since 2nd class. Nice in their own way, but don't expect them to have you in stitches of laughter. They were the cautious one on your Leaving Cert holiday. I suppose every gang needs one of them!

**The Annoying Parent.** This person just wants to talk about their kids all the way through the Zoom banter. The more wine they get into them, the more they will talk about their kids. Now, nothing wrong with loving your children, of course, but do you think that your single mates, who can't get out on the town to have some fun and meet people, want to hear about how good little Jimmy is at wiping his own arse now? Of course they don't. The same person will drag one of their kids into the screen and embarrass them by asking them to sing a song, or to tell mammy's friends how good her banana bread is.

**The One with the Crap Internet.** Every Zoom quiz night had this person, who comes in and out of the Zoom for the whole night due to crappy Internet. So annoying when you're in the middle of a quiz or a chat and this one keeps

coming in and out, or would start talking and
– bang – screen frozen, then everyone trying to
tell them that they're frozen, but their Internet
would come back on just as they finished telling
a story, with a 'Do yous know what I mean?' No,
we don't, because your Internet is absolutely
brutal. Sort it out and upgrade or you're barred
from our Zoom nights.

**The Covid Worrier.** Everyone of course had
Covid in the back of their minds during these
lockdowns, but Friday night was a switch-off
period to log on to your Zoom for a quiz and
forget about what was happening. There was
always one, though, who just worried above
and beyond. No matter what the topic of
conversation would be, this poor divil would
always go back to Covid. 'Ah, but the numbers
today were very high,' or 'My friend's cousin
said that pubs won't open back up till 2024,
and there will be no planes leaving Ireland till
summer 2023 at the earliest unless they are
going to China to get us more PPE gear.' They
often had to be told to stop talking about Covid
or they would be removed from the Zoom.

**The Laid-Back Head.** You could listen to this
person all night! No matter how bad things

were or seemed, this person was having none of it and was always looking on the bright side of everything. Nothing fazed them, they paid no attention to the news, and just rolled with it. Always good having this person on an auld Zoom quiz to boost morale.

**The Pisshead.** They had absolutely no interest in the quiz, just wanted to go on the beer as best as they could with company, even if the company was through a laptop. They would get bored of the quiz very quickly, and would often say, 'Don't mind the quiz, load of shit, anyone know any good drinking games?' They were usually the first or last to log off, depending on how much drink they had in the house. The morning after the night before, the standard text from this person would land into the group WhatsApp: 'Listen, sorry about last night. I'd had a long week, I didn't mean to waffle and say what I did, especially to you, Pauline. I do like you, the wine just got to my head. MiWadi for me next Friday. Chat soon girls, love yas'. Then of course history would always repeat itself the following Friday!

## Stories from the public

*My missus used my card to pay for puppy school over Zoom and made me sit through it. One-on-one with a trainer and the dog over Zoom would be insane enough, but it was a split screen with seven other clowns and their pups. And the dog still humps my work boots.*

*(Justin M.)*

# Bingo in the flats

One positive thing that the pandemic brought out was a sense of community. Pre-Covid times, you could have passed your neighbour every day and barely said hello to them, but because everyone was experiencing such weird times, a smile and a conversation were very important. Yes, it was probably the same conversation every time you walked by your neighbours' garden – 'Lovely day,' 'God, we'll appreciate normal times when they come back,' 'The numbers are very high,' etc. – but it was a conversation nonetheless. Especially for elderly people who lived by themselves and just had medication and food dropped off to them on a weekly basis. They craved a bit of human interaction. Postal workers played a huge part in this, especially out in the countryside. Believe it or not, the sound of the pebbles crunching on the driveway and the sight of the An Post van was as exciting as the day got for many elderly people. All they would want was five minutes of the postman's time to have a chat.

Some communities really went all out to have a bit of craic and not let Covid get in the way. The residents of Ringsend in Dublin were a perfect example of that: the local folk there decided that people needed something to look forward to, so they set up 'Bingo in the flats'. In the evening, everyone would come out onto their balcony and play bingo.

There was a fella high up on a rooftop with a sound system calling out the numbers while the youth dropped cards around to each flat. This was brilliant, because it gave everyone something to look forward to, and I'm sure it gave them a sense that they were in it together. Class idea. Mind you, a bit like the Zoom quizzes, I'm sure the folk of Ringsend had their fair share of bingo from the flats by the end of it, but no doubt it got many of them through a very difficult few months in their lives. Hard to beat the bond of a tight-knit community.

# Clapping for the nurses

Do you remember the evening we all stood out in our front gardens and clapped the nurses for all the hard work they had been doing during the pandemic? We felt we had to do something to show our gratitude for the hard work that all the nurses and doctors around the country were doing during these unforeseen times.

It was actually quite funny, the whole thing. We were living with my parents at the time. As far as I can remember, it was about eight o'clock when everyone had to come out and clap. Lots of people were full of wine or a few beers, so everyone, on my mam's road anyway, was in great form, clapping away, with the odd 'G'wan the nurses.' Everyone was afraid to go too close to each other, so there were full-blown conversations from one garden to the next.

Only in Ireland would you see this: two ladies in a deep and meaningful conversation 25 feet away from each other and then one says, 'Pauline, hold on there until I go in and get me glass of wine.' So the clapping for the nurses turned into many a housing estate out having chats with each other about how mad things were. Not only did the nurses and healthcare workers get a clap, but neighbours got to have a chat with each other in person, albeit from a fair distance away. It was a chat all the same, though, which is always good for the auld noggin!

# The Meath ladies

Sport was badly missed during the tight lockdowns. When it initially came back it was great, but it just wasn't the same without the supporters. So, many teams got a warm welcome in 2021.

One match I was at in 2021 that had an unbelievable atmosphere was the All-Ireland Ladies' Senior Football Final between Meath and Dublin in Croke Park. Now you can call me biased if you want, but it was one of the best sporting performances I have ever witnessed in my life from Meath – they were just unreal. Nobody gave them a chance going into the final against this all-conquering Dublin outfit, who were chasing five titles in a row. But the gallant Meath ladies didn't read the pre-match script and played the game on their own terms. These are ladies who lost the intermediate final in 2018 and 2019, then won it at the third time of asking in 2020, and the very next year got to the holy grail of ladies' football.

This bunch of girls are a credit, not just to their clubs or county, but to the whole country. The lift this gave to ladies' sport in the country is up there with Katie Taylor, Kellie Harrington and Leona Maguire. A group of heroes, who are hopefully only getting started ... Up Meath!

# Chapter 4:
# The Hard Times

# Our Covid experience

Even though I wrote this book to share my own experiences of the pandemic and the lighter side of it all, it wouldn't feel right if I didn't cover the sad and devastating side of those scary times also. No doubt some people reading this book have lost a loved one, not just to Covid-19, but it was terrible during the lockdown times when no one could come to pay their respects. I think at one stage only six people were allowed at funerals, and there was no such thing as a wake. As you and I both know, one thing we Irish have always been great at is giving each other a proper send-off.

Normally, in the two days' build-up to the funeral, the deceased's house would be full of family and neighbours coming to pay their respects. Tea and sandwiches everywhere, drink, cakes, chicken curries and salads. People telling stories around the coffin to make others laugh at the toughest of times. This was all part and parcel of the early grieving period, but not during the strict lockdowns. It must have been so hard for some people to cope.

Covid hit a lot of houses over those two years. A lot of families got it mild, and the isolation was the hardest part, but some were not so lucky and were very sick – or worse. My own house experienced our slice of it in March 2021. My wife Emma contracted it around Paddy's Day, and it fairly knocked her back. She, like most women, is hardy, and wouldn't complain unless she really wasn't well – unlike me, I suppose, who would play the dying swan with a head cold.

But she defo wasn't well with it. Our little daughter Lucy, who was only four months old at the time, also picked it up, and herself and Emma were trying to isolate up in the bedroom. But try telling a two-year-old toddler to stay away from his mother. Sure, when I wasn't looking, Zach would gallop up the stairs, barge through the door and leap up on the bed beside her. Not just that, he would grab Lucy's soother out of her mouth and stick it in his own gob and make his way into his own bedroom. We'd no hope. I'm sure plenty of houses can relate to that scenario!

But after about seven days of having it, Emma took a turn for the worse, and we had to ring an ambulance for her, following the local GP's advice. I won't lie, it was one of the toughest things I've had to witness:

my own wife, my best friend, being taken away in an ambulance with Covid-19 while myself and the three kids stood there at the front door, helpless. As you can imagine, every bad thought went through my mind, you know the way. You would have heard plenty of stories like, 'Did ya hear of that young person with no underlying conditions who died of Covid?' So I was extremely nervous, to be honest.

The worst about this poxy virus was that nobody could help you. In normal circumstances, my parents would have come down to the house and helped me with the little ones, but this couldn't happen, as we couldn't take the risk of them picking up the virus. So I was left alone with three young kids, and with little Lucy already positive I was bound to get it.

After 24 hours of struggle, I rang my dad and told him straight that I couldn't cope. The thing that worried me the most was the little man, Zach. He was running riot in the house, and I wasn't able to keep an eye on him because I was up to my eyes with Lucy. I'd say I changed more nappies in that week than I had for the previous two children put together. I was as far out of my comfort zone as I've ever been!

We needed to figure out who had Covid, so a private on-call person came out and did tests on us.

I came back positive, but Ella and Zach were still negative, so we made a decision that we were going to get Zach out of the house and up to my parents, just to relieve some pressure. We had to get a PCR test just to confirm I was defo positive and the two kids weren't, so my father came down to mind Lucy while we did this.

I'll never forget the head on him when I opened the front door. He stood there with, I'm not messing, about seven masks on, all wrapped around his head, nose, ears – you name it, he had it covered. I'd say my mam togged him out! He gave me a little laugh at the most perfect time.

And then when he came into the house, I warned him that Lucy had Covid, and to stay clear of her as best he could. She was asleep in her buggy, so my father opened up the back door, stood out in the cold and pushed the buggy, with just his hand inside and the rest of his body outside with his head leaned as far away from her as possible. It was gas to look at.

I told him he should really have gloves on in case the virus was on the handle of the buggy. He told me not to worry, that he came prepared, and he proceeded to take a pair of big dirty garden gloves out of his arse pocket and stick them on – the bang of dirty soil off them and all! That gave me another laugh.

I'm raging that I wasn't in the headspace to get a photo of him. It would have been gas to look back on, but it reconfirmed for me again that laughing is the best thing for you, as it relieved a bit of stress. It's funny, I had Covid and felt absolutely dirt with it, but because of the situation I was in I wasn't able to allow myself to feel crap, so it just shows the power of the mind when ya really need it.

There were two or three days where I was floored altogether, and thankfully we were able to call on

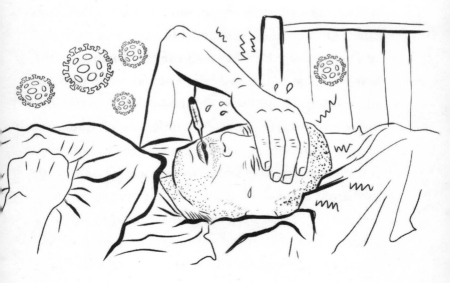

my sister-in-law Shauna to come over and take the baby off me for a few hours so I could get some sleep. She was just out of isolation herself, so she was able to come into the house. That was a big help. The neighbours helping out was also some boost. Friends are great like that, all giving each other a dig-out. I must give a special mention to Janet Durkan, a family friend who, when it was so badly needed in the house, dropped down a feed of McDonald's and left it at the door and off she went. It meant a lot to me at that time. It's the little things that mean a lot when you're going through a tough time, no doubt about that!

So, eight very worrying and up-and-down days later, Emma finally arrived home from hospital. I can't describe the relief when she got in the door and was on the mend. It had been such a horrible couple of weeks, but it really landed home with me that this virus was a real thing, and it's only when it does land at your doorstop and affects a loved one as badly as it did Emma, that you begin to see the truly scary side of the pandemic.

# Mental health

Social isolation was a big barrier for many during those days. It was especially tough if you lived by yourself. Anyone who had never experienced a mental health issue I'd imagine did during the pandemic, and for those who suffered on a regular basis with their mental well-being, this was survival mode! I tried to use my platform to raise awareness on this, just little posts reminding people that it's OK not to feel OK, and it's OK to feel low and worried, but to not keep it to themselves and to talk about it: pick up the phone, call down to a neighbour, stand in their garden and have a real conversation about how you're feeling. I firmly believe that talking is the number-one best medicine for your well-being – being honest and straight up about what's going on in your mind.

I defo had plenty of bad days during the lockdowns. I have always been very open about my mental health. I suppose, like many, it was the unknown that weighed me down, especially in the industry I'm in: live entertainment! I was worried this game might never get going again, and after the hard work I'd put in to get to where I was, it now looked like it was being flushed down the toilet. It is key to not let your mind run away with itself, and as humans we're woeful at that, picking the negative over the positive. It was all about staying in the moment and, when you got bogged down with your inner thoughts, picking up the phone and chatting to someone. Or you could get some exercise in, move the body. That was key for me, anyway!

It was tough times for everyone, and talking about their true feelings was how folk got by. If anything positive has come out of the pandemic, it's that mental-health awareness has come to the forefront. We're not fully there yet, but I feel that, because of what everyone has been through over the past couple of years, people are a little bit more comfortable being honest about how they feel, and I hope the stigma around it vanishes completely over the next few years. It simply has to.

# Chapter 5: Me, Myself and I – Self-Improvement

# Home workouts

With no gyms open or team sports allowed during the lockdowns, lots of us took to home workouts – not just the fitness heads but also folks who hadn't had any decent exercise since PE in school gave it a lash. The reason for this was a mixture of absolute boredom and feeling the need to burn some of the calories they were putting into the tank.

Joe Wicks was the main man when it came to the home workouts. He seems like a great guy in fairness, and lots of people enjoyed his workouts on YouTube. He always brought fun to the table. A special mention also should go to T.J. Reid, the Kilkenny legend who runs T.J. Reid Health and Fitness, who also took to Facebook Live to do PE for youngsters of all ages and sizes all over the country. All you needed was a hurl and a ball. Some of the youth got great enjoyment out of that.

With gym equipment and proper weights hard to come by, we all had to use our imaginations: tins of beans, tins of paint, two-litre bottles of water, or in some houses a two-litre of cider – so it was there to have a sup after, to 'reward yourself'. Myself and my daughter did our own workout videos in the back garden. We would just set up a few stations and do different bodyweight stuff at each. It was fun, kept us busy and I think a few people copied our workouts and did them in their own gardens with their kids, which is all positive. We weren't on Joe Wicks' level, but it was enjoyable all the same, and good bonding time with my little lady.

Speaking of home workouts, how could I talk about the lockdowns and not talk about these 5k runs that became very popular? I'm not sure how – again, boredom I suppose – but these became a big thing. Everyone was doing them and posting up their times on social media. The likes of football teams would be doing them to stay fit and sending their times into the WhatsApp group to impress the manager and show him that you meant business for when the season finally got up and running again. But you see, the real elephant in the room on this topic was the outrageous cheating that was going on – *you know who you are.*

Lads would be posting sub-20-minute times for their 5k's, and these were the same lads who when playing football would be bolloxed after a couple of laps of the field, who would be leaving the local Centra with an eight-pack of cans five days a week – would ya stop! See, with these Fitbits and fancy apps you can head off on your 5k run, stop the clock whenever you feel like it, scratch the arse, have an ice cream, chat away to someone and just press start again and continue on.

It was funny, though, when you saw people out running and a gang of people would be coming towards them. They would up the tempo like Mo Farah (look at me, I'm a brilliant runner) and then collapse around the corner once everyone was out of sight and begin to walk then for a few minutes. Anyways, as I always preach, exercise is a powerful tool for your mental health, so keep up the running – just be honest with your times!

# Sea swimming

Sea swimming became a huge thing during the pandemic. Even Matt Damon and his SuperValu bag got in on the action. If you're not into it you would think people are crazy, and I don't blame you. Like, think about it for a minute: you're getting up at the crack of dawn, leaving your warm, cosy bed and making your way to the seaside. And as you and I both know, the Irish seaside is not like Spain or Portugal; it's rough and ready. Especially during the winter months, it can be very, very sharp, the sand hard and often rocky, the Baltic temperatures in the water. When you put it like that, only the half-mad people would put themselves through it. I have to admit I am one of those half-mad people, and I got into it even more during the pandemic.

Only people who are into it will understand the positives to it, like talk about the mental health benefits! When you get into that cold Irish seawater, that initial agony feels like you're being stabbed all over your body, and not an inch of your skin avoids that pain! The mind is going absolutely bonkers, telling you to 'get the fuck out of here', not to mention the poor man downstairs about to fall off you!

But once you get through that initial sting and pain, after a few minutes it starts to ease, and as you control your mind it can become enjoyable. And when you leave the water and get yourself dry and warm, that's when the real benefit hits you. (A good tip is to bring a few litres of lukewarm water and put your feet and hands into it after – top class, the auld body will be warm again in no time.) The freshness in both your body and mind is priceless and is certainly worth that bit of pain when you first enter the water. Even invest in one of them dryrobes – the big long coats – they are the business and heat ya up fairly quickly.

I do most of my sea swimming down in Bettystown Beach in Co. Meath of a Sunday morning. There does be a gang of women who are there every single Sunday morning first thing. I actually think some of them go every single morning of the week, for that matter. Honest to God, you can just feel the positive vibes off them each time. They're all in great form, all as mad as a box of frogs, but the salt of the earth, as hardy a bunch of women as you will find. Always slagging myself about the videos and that. I'm sure they've had a glimpse of my spotty arse on a few occasions – can't imagine they'd bother taking a selfie with that view, anyway!

What sea swimming does for your mental health is top-notch, and I would defo encourage anyone who may be suffering with their mental well-being since the pandemic to give it a lash. As the old saying goes, 'Don't diss it until you've tried it.' I know it's not for everyone, but the benefits are huge, trust me.

Sure g'wan, give it a go and 'sea'! You can thank me later!

# DIY

During the first lockdown everyone was trying to find stuff to do around the house and the garden. It was a good chance to clear out clutter in the house and get things done that you might never have had the chance to do otherwise. Washing windows, painting fences, cutting grass – even when it didn't need to be cut it was getting done anyway.

We were all looking for small jobs around the house to keep the mind from going crazy. Here's one story that sums it up for you. So myself and my dad, Joe, would enjoy a game of golf, and with all golf courses closed during the lockdowns we were thinking of how we might be able to get our fix! We had many a chipping competition out in the back garden, chipping into a bucket, nothing too fancy, just basic! It was nearly a Friday-evening tradition for a few weeks. We'd have the dinner with a few glasses of wine, then head out the back for a chipping competition and a sup of a few cold ones under the evening sky. But if you played golf with me, you wouldn't think I'd spent a lockdown practising chipping. I'm still fairly useless at it – it breaks my heart!

Anyways, after a couple weeks of chipping we began to get bored, so we tried to think up other ways to hit a few golf balls. We had been looking everywhere online for a driving net, so we could set it up in the back garden and smash balls into it, but no matter where we looked, they were sold out. The world was in lockdown, to be fair, and there was more than one Tiger Woods wannabe out there craving some sort of golf fix.

So we decided to have a go at making our own home-made one. My father, being handy, decided that, with the right material, he would be able to build us a good one, and we could hit golf balls into it to our hearts' content! Joe said that if we were going to make one, we may as well make a big one: ten foot high by ten foot wide so we couldn't possibly miss it!

Off we went then, down to the local hardware store. We had a vision of getting a massive lump of plywood, stapling artificial grass to it and hanging a bed sheet in front of that. In theory, it sounded genius and wouldn't have cost half the money a good one online would have. Emma did give her opinion that she didn't think it would work, but like two thick men we disagreed and powered on with our project.

We bought the material and spent the morning putting it together. If anything, at least it passed a few hours, which wasn't an easy thing to do during those days! Both of us were very excited, thinking this was going to be like playing the Augusta National (where the US Masters is held). That's how much we craved some sort of a game of golf, or even just to be able to pull on a golf ball with a seven iron!

When it was ready, we put it up against the neighbours' wall and got out a few golf balls. We did rock paper scissors to see who had the honour of taking the first tee shot off our state-of-the-art home-made driving range! I won with a solid rock, so with pure excitement, I took no club other than the driver out of the bag, teed up my Pro V1 golf ball, took a practice swing and then a deep breath to focus and, imagining I was on the first hole at Ashbourne Golf Club (my local course), let rip!

As soon as I made connection, my heart sank, as the ball hopped off the plywood, came straight back at me and nearly took my head off. I ducked, and it hit the neighbours' wall, came back and hit my parents' window and left a lovely crack! The look of anger and disappointment on my father's face …

That was the end of our driving range after just one shot. All that excitement, ambition, effort and commitment to get it, already gone down the swanny! Not for the first time, my wife was right when I had a left-field idea. So it was back to chipping for myself and the auld lad until the golf courses reopened.

# Writing sketches

I spent a lot of the lockdowns making sketches. When live events couldn't seem further away, I was thinking to myself, 'Just your luck, when you start to get going at the comedy, it looks like live entertainment has gone belly up.' I had just done a very successful tour in 2019 and looked at it as a springboard to drive on with tours. I, like plenty of performers, had my 2020 calendar completely cleared, and there was nothing anybody could do about it. Like most, I started to feel sorry for myself, but the way I look at life in general is that you have two options: you can either sit on your hands or you can roll up your sleeves, no matter what situation arises.

So, I thought to myself, with the country at a standstill and stuck mainly in their homes, it meant online activity would go through the roof, as in everyone would be scrolling through social media the whole time. I looked at it as an opportunity, I suppose, to get my name out there a bit more. I began doing daily sketches based on what was currently happening in the country. Nothing major, no groundbreaking comedy, just simple little relatable sketches that everyone could look at and see either themselves or someone they knew in them.

So myself and the family came up with ideas each day. I got a massive help off a friend called Neil Doherty, the local postman who delivers the post to my mam's housing estate. A big GAA man, originally from Cabra in Dublin, and a gas man, a typical Dub, very witty. He has always been a fan of the sketches and was at a couple of my shows and book launches over the years, a real salt-of-the-earth-type fella. So he was my right-hand man for the 'Covid content'.

He would finish delivering his post by lunchtime (don't tell his boss that!), meaning he would be free in the afternoon to make the sketches. Jesus, we made some amount of them. One thing I noticed was the feedback; it was never as positive. Usually, I'd get the bit of negativity under my posts, which is standard, but for whatever reason, these Covid sketches were getting 99 per cent positive feedback. People couldn't get enough of them.

Did I feel a bit of pressure to keep producing them? I did, to be honest, and the odd time I'd get a bit bogged down and stressed when I couldn't come up with a fresh idea, and my mam would often say,

'Rory, take a day off, you'll burn yourself out. People will understand. Sure you've made one, sometimes two, a day for the past few weeks.'

And she was right, but the way I looked at it, doctors and nurses were working harder than they ever had before to help save lives in the hospitals, and on paper my occupation is to make people laugh, so I felt I needed to do that to the best of my ability during these scary times for people.

It has to be said, some of the craic we had making them was brilliant, especially the ones taking the piss out of the Garda checkpoints. One question I always get asked, both online and in person, is 'How did ya manage to get your hands on the Garda uniform?'

Well, I'll tell you exactly how. A few years ago, I was doing a GAA-themed stand-up show in various GAA clubs around the country. I finished a gig one night in a club (I won't name the club, for obvious reasons!), and just as I was getting into my car a man shouted at me to hold on a minute, and he went to the boot of his car. He then came over to me with this big black bag. I didn't know what was in it, maybe some old GAA jerseys he was giving me for a few GAA skits. But he went on to tell me that he was an ex-guard, and he had a bit of uniform lying around the house and said I could have it if I wanted to do a few skits on the police force!

His exact words were, 'Here Rory, go have a bit of craic with that. Lord Jaysus, there is plenty of piss to be taken out of us guards!' I gladly took the gear off him, thanked him, threw the bag into the back of my car and off I went. I remember thinking to myself as I left those GAA grounds, 'Happy Christmas! I am going to have some craic with this.'

Whenever we would be doing the Garda sketches it used to be gas seeing the heads on people and their reactions when they saw us in the Garda uniform. You know how us Irish just shit ourselves when we see guards, even if you'd have done nothing wrong, you just feel like you have. So I would see the fear in people's eyes when they saw me togged out, especially if we were doing a checkpoint sketch.

A car would come around the corner, and once they knew it wasn't a real guard they were faced with, the window would go down and a roar would come out, 'Ya messing bollox, ya. I was shitting myself there for a minute. This car is out of tax, and I was coming up with a world of excuses to tell ye guards. G'wan ya messer ya, keep up the videos!' And off they would go.

One day in between the lockdowns, when the pubs were open but had to close by 10 p.m., myself and a couple of friends went over to a pub in Ratoath (a neighbouring parish of mine) to have a couple of scoops – we craved a few creamy pints of stout at this stage.

It wasn't a minute past 10 p.m. and in came the guards to clear the place out. It was weird, because nobody was doing anything crazy wrong, just having a few drinks, but at this time all pubs were meant to be empty at 10 p.m. So, typical me, as the guards were in one side of the pub shouting, 'Right, c'mon now, everyone out. Put down your drinks and out yous go,' I got a brainwave of a sketch idea!

During them days I always carried the Garda uniform in the boot of my car, in case an opportunity arose, just like this one. So out I ran to the car and grabbed the jacket and hat, threw them on and back in I went. As I was walking in through the side door there was a guard there talking to two young lads telling them to finish off their cigarettes and move on. One of them copped me and said, 'Go on ya boy ya, Rory's Stories,' and the three of them looked around at me. I was half expecting the guard to arrest me for having the Garda gear on me, but he said, 'Whatever video you're making in there, I didn't see ya and make it quick!' This guard must have been a fan of the sketches! So in I went and recreated what had just happened and threw it up online the next day.

I suppose that's always the way with the videos. The best ones are often the ones I don't plan. I just get the inspiration from real-life scenarios. It's just like a savage night out – the ones you don't plan are the best!

# My *Ultimate Hell Week* experience

Back in September 2020 I was sitting on the couch and I got an email from a woman called Jen Searle. She was asking me if I would be interested in taking part in a 'celebrity' (not mad on that word!) *Special Forces: Ultimate Hell Week*. I was already a fan of this show. I had been glued to the first two seasons of it, and found it brilliant viewing, so raw and so real. When watching it, myself and Emma would often talk about if we could do it, or how far we thought we would go. I said if I ever got the chance I would defo do it, as it would be a savage experience.

Well, mocking is catching, and be careful what you wish for, because here I was in the middle of being in real-life *Hell Week* with the lockdowns, and now I was being asked to take part in the show. Jen said that the feedback when they had been asking people to take part had been 'Hell yeah' or 'Not a hope.' I thought about it for a bit, and then decided to meet up with Jen for more details. We met in the Ashbourne House Hotel in my home town and discussed what the show was going to be like. Like I expected, she said it was as raw and real as you could imagine. She advised me to get training hard, get used to carrying heavy weight on my back and get used to cold water, as I would be in it a lot!

One question I did raise at the time was about the combat fighting. I had seen on previous shows that men had to fight women, and there were no ifs or buts. I explained to her that I would do anything asked of me bar fight a woman. I just wouldn't have it in me, and also, back in 2018 I got some backlash on Twitter over a sketch I made, and I wasn't willing to step into a ring on national TV and fight a woman with the potential that I could be on the receiving end of more backlash. Jen said she understood and would flag that. Anyways, I agreed then and there that I was gonna take part. It was due to be filmed in mid-November, so I had about eight or nine weeks to somewhat get my body ready for this. I was scared and excited at the same time.

I hooked up with two good lads I train with, Tony Burke and Wayne McGrath, both qualified personal trainers, to get me in as best a shape we could for this madness. But unfortunately, a couple of weeks into the training, the country went back into Level 5 lockdown and the date in November had to be postponed, as the rules were that filming would not be permitted by the powers-that-be to take place while the country was in Level 5 restrictions. This went on for ages. The original start date was postponed until further notice.

But back in October 2020, the desire to eat well and train like a dog was gone out the window for the moment, so I went on and enjoyed my Christmas, while keeping the training going, just not as intense.

I was training very well until mid-March when our house got hit hard with Covid and I couldn't do anything physical for nearly four weeks. But with all the hardship that was going on in that scary time, I no doubt was working on my mental strength! I suppose you couldn't have trained for the experience I went through with Emma and the Covid. So, without knowing at the time, it would stand to me, because at the end of the day what I was signing myself up for was a TV show, when that ordeal was a real-life hell week!

When everyone was back to normal after all the Covid had left the house and I started to get energy back, I had four weeks to do as much as I could to be ready for this madness that was coming my way! The two lads, Wayne and Tony, got it fairly spot on. In a situation like this, with time not exactly on our side, rest was just as important as training. So we would train hard one day and rest and stretch the next day.

We did that for the four weeks, and I even went off the drink (well, maybe the odd bottle of a Saturday night, but in general I was as dry as a cracker!). Our training consisted of a mix of personal training sessions in the gym, with the lads putting me through very intense 90-minute workouts. I asked them to push me every single time and treat me like a piece of shit, because that's how these DS's (the

'Directing Staff', as the show had them called) were going to treat me: have zero respect for me, call me a useless prick, all ya want. I'm sure the lads got great enjoyment out of that. We would go to Bettystown Beach, run up and down a few sand dunes and then into the water – loads and loads of time in the Irish Sea. The body needed to get used to that!

Myself and Wayne did a lot of training up in the Hill of Tara. I'd bring my backpack, load it with up to 25kg. We'd walk for a good half hour or so, then there's this dirty hill at the bottom of the Hill of Tara that most of the great Meath teams would have run up and down during pre-season. It's horrible tough, even for the fittest of people.

Wayne had me running up and down that hill carrying the backpack until I was sick. It was without question the hardest training I have ever done. He'd be shouting in my ear, saying anything and everything to piss me off and to try get the absolute best out of me. It was a great place to lay it all out. Only Meath folk will know what I mean when I say there is something special about the Hill of Tara, something spiritual about the place.

And when I was walking back down the hill, looking out over the beautiful green fields, breathing out of my arse, I often felt like I was going to be representing my county by doing this show. I knew I was the only Meath person taking part, and I didn't want to let the county down. Meath has always been known as a never-say-die county on the football field, and I wanted to carry that attitude into *Hell Week*. I flogged myself on that hill many a time in preparation for the torture that was coming my way.

After four intense and enjoyable (not sure if that's the right word to use!) weeks of training with the lads, the time had come to hit the road and head for *Hell Week*. I already had some motivation heading down, provided by my father. Before I left, Emma said to me, 'Your da was up here the other day and said that he might book a hotel room near Cork and wait there for a night. No point in driving down to Cork with Rory, he said, driving back and having to go back down the next day and collect him because he got thick with a sergeant or that.'

That was just the motivation I needed heading down. No matter what happened, dead or alive, I was lasting more than one day down there to prove him wrong. Nothing like fathers and sons hopping off each other.

I got ready to go to Cork, a kiss for the kids and a kiss and a hug for Emma. She knew I wasn't doing this for any extra fame or exposure or any bullshit like that. I was doing this to see how far I could push myself to gain valuable life experience and learn something about myself. I told her that, unless I came home in an ambulance, she wouldn't be seeing me for a few days. She knows better than anyone how pig determined I can be when I put my mind to something. I had her full backing.

With a big bag full of clothes, plasters, Vaseline, inhalers and about 37 pairs of socks, off I went to Cork, to take part in what was going to be one of the best experiences of my life. We were meeting in the Vienna Woods Hotel in Glanmire. The plan was to go straight to our rooms, where someone came and did a Covid test. Once that came back negative it was all systems go.

After the Covid test, we got a full going-over by the medics and doctor, so they could confirm that they felt our bodies were up for the chaos that was coming our way. After that, I got a knock on the door, and it was somebody with the clothes that I was to wear throughout my time on *Hell Week*. All XL, of course. I tried them on, and nothing really fitted me, especially the trousers. They were up my hole. I was afraid to even do a squat in them in case they burst.

Not to worry, I rang Jen, and she came up, took the clothes off me and said she would be back up with XXL gear. I waited in the room for about a half hour until a knock on the door came. I opened it and it was Jen again, standing there holding all my crumpled-up clothes. 'I'm so sorry, Rory, but these are the largest clothes we have. You're going to have to make do with them.'

'Absolutely fucking marvellous,' I thought to myself. What a start, heading off to *Hell Week* with trousers too small for me, an easy target for their DS.

Later that evening, all the recruits met downstairs in our gear to go to our photo shoot. I hadn't met any of them before bar Darran O'Sullivan, a really good fella. We had chatted plenty pre-*Hell Week* about training and all. We were all introduced to each other and off we went for the photo shoot. You could sense the fear in the air. Everyone was really giddy, some trying to crack jokes, but in general, you knew everyone was shitting themselves deep down.

When that was all out of the way we made our way back to the hotel, got our 'final supper' and were told to be down at hotel reception, in our normal clothes, our uniform packed in a bag and ready to rock at 4 a.m.

That morning we were all there, nibbling at bits and pieces of breakfast. Then, nerves galore, off we went outside and loaded onto the bus. The bus was all blacked out, so we had no idea where we were going. Peter Stringer had a sort of satnav on his phone and was trying to make heads or tails of where we were off to. As we got close to our destination, Jen asked for our phones, put them in a big bag and called out our names to give us our numbers.

'Rory … Number 13.' A roar went up, 'Haha! Unlucky for some, Rory, whaaa.'

So that was me. I would be known as Number 13 for the foreseeable future. At this stage, everyone was rattled. I was sitting with Darran on the bus, and I turned to him and said, 'This is what it must feel like on the morning of an All-Ireland Final' and Darran totally disagreed with me. He said, 'Yerra, not at all. This is way worse. At least with a football match, you have a fair idea of what's going to happen. With this, I've fucking no clue. Way worse, man – I'm bricking it.'

I felt the same way. A gig brings nerves, but at least you're in control of it in some way. But this, this was a whole different ball game. Nobody had a clue what was about to happen.

Jen said, 'From now on, it's just yourselves. You can't make any contact with me or any of the production team. Best of luck.' And off the bus she went.

We got a bang on the door a couple of minutes later and one by one we exited the bus. We were in the most beautiful surroundings of Cork, Roberts Cove. It was bright, calm and just stunning, until I saw a man over on the beach wearing a balaclava and with 18 life jackets in front of him. 'Here we go!' I thought to myself.

He shouted at us all to line up, put on the jackets and start walking towards a couple of boats that we could see in the distance on the water. We started walking out, in our full clothes. The water was baltic. It was some buzz all the same. I could hear nothing but the splish-splash of us as we made our way towards these boats. I had a few words with myself, like, 'Well Rory, this is it now. Things are gonna get very wild very soon – but you're ready!'

We jumped on these speedboats and started flying around the harbour. We were all freezing at this stage with the wet clothes on us, not knowing what the hell was going on. Then we heard a helicopter behind us and turned around and there was the head of Ray Goggins, eyeballing us from the chopper. It was freaky. This went on for what felt like hours until eventually the boat made its way in a different direction.

We pulled up to this pier and I could see some of the familiar DS faces from the shows I had watched. They were waiting for us, and let's just say they weren't exactly smiling with 99s in their hands! They roared at us: 'Get out of the fucking boats – quick!'

Panic stations straight away. I leapt out of the boat and nearly cracked my head off a rock, swallowed a gallon of seawater and got up the pier as best I could with soaking wet clothes on me. Some start!

We all ran in single file, with very angry Alsatian dogs on leashes barking at us. We were told to line up with our backs against the wall and sit down in a squat position. Never felt a burn like it before in my legs, and as we were hanging there, these madmen in all black were roaring and shouting at us.

It's honestly hard to describe how intense that moment was. You went from zero to 500 miles an hour within seconds. Then we were told to strip down to our briefs and follow them. We got to the bottom of these steps, and they rang a bell and we were made to go up about 170 steps in total, all straight uphill and into the dark. This was known as 'go ring the bell', and horrible isn't even the word for it. Legs hanging and chest exploding going up those stairs.

This environment I found myself in was without question the absolute furthest I have ever been out of my comfort zone. I remember when we were lined up beside our beds, looking over at the likes of Peter Stringer, Melanie Nocher, Andrew Trimble, all professional athletes by trade, and here's me, who lined out for his club's Junior B team earlier that year! But I did calm my inner voice by reassuring myself that these people may not have been to the dark places I have in life, the real low places (though I'm sure they had, as professional sport can be cut-throat) but I used this to tell myself that I had good mental strength and was used to feeling shite and dragging myself back up off the ground.

I remember Ray Goggins walking into the room. The presence that man carries is hard to describe. He's like a real-life action man. He laid down the law with us. One thing I remember him saying was, 'I don't know why some of yous are here, to rejuvenate a failed career or whatever.' And I remember saying to myself that's not why I'm here. I'm happy with where *Rory's Stories* is at the minute. I've worked hard for what I have, so that's not my reason for being here. I'm here for myself. I'm not going to compare myself to anyone else in this room. It's me against me, and that's it.

The first pass/fail event we did was jumping out of a helicopter, and I actually found that grand, to be honest with you. It didn't scare me at all, really. I did, mind you, have to hold a heavy whoor of a rock over my head for a decent spell, because Ger Reidy saw I had a bracelet on me and no jewellery was allowed on the course. I wouldn't mind but I never wear jewellery and only had it on because it represented a mental health charity called 'Need to Talk?', but Reidy copped it and labelled me the 'Jewellery Man', and that was it. In fairness to him, the public got a good laugh out of that when the show aired. One witty man is Ger!

We lost Eamon McGee and Paul Olima to the helicopter jump, which was too bad, as we could have done with the two lads' brute strength as the days went on. It just shows ya, fear is a real thing, and the lads struggled with heights and water, and unfortunately, that was them gone. A pity, especially

Eamon, as I liked him as a footballer, a hard, dirty solid full-back who I'm sure would have gone far if that event hadn't been the first one on the cards, but that's *Hell Week* for you. It will get you out of your comfort zone one way or another, and test you to your absolute limits!

For anyone who watched the show and thought, 'Oh sure, they must get a break when the cameras are off them,' unfortunately not. From the minute you get there until the minute you hand over your armband, it's 100 miles an hour. When you're watching it on RTÉ every Wednesday night for six weeks you forget that it was all recorded over five days – madness!

I had lots of ups and downs on the show, even on the first day, when I was the only one who wasn't able to climb up the side of the ship. Listen, it was always going to be very difficult for myself, with the weight that I am and all that. It's not an ideal event for me. I remember sitting in the little speedboat on that dirty, windy and wet day, watching people getting up into the boat one by one, and thinking to myself, 'This is not gonna be good.'

I was going OK until I cramped in the hamstring, and that was the end of that – white flag. In any other environment, if you attempt something and fail you will usually get a 'Hard luck,' or a 'You did your best, well done.' Not in this world; in *Hell Week* there's no such thing as praise! In fact, it's quite the opposite. When the DS see you struggling at something they will let you know. It's all part of the game to try to break you!

After failing to climb up the side of the ship, the demons were in full flow in my mind as I stood facing the wall, saying, 'You're useless, Rory. What are ya doing here, ya clown? You don't deserve to be here. You're the only one who didn't get up the ship, you let the whole team down.'

All these negative thoughts were racing around my mind, but one thing I have learned over time is bouncebackability, and anyone who has read my memoir, *Rory's Story*, will know what I mean. I was used to beating myself up mentally, it's nothing new to me, but I also always knew that I was capable of bouncing back when I fall down, and that's what *Hell Week* was, a pure test of resilience – testing how many times you can fall and get back up again. So as much as the demons were wreaking havoc in my mind after failing to climb up the side of the ship, I knew I had it in me deep down to rise again. There was no hope of me handing over my band and going home. I wouldn't be able to live with myself if I did that.

After doing a stupid amount of exercise from about 6 a.m. that first morning, we still had had zero sleep by 1.30 a.m. the following morning. And don't even get me started on the food, that was a killer altogether – well for me personally, who, as you can imagine, loves his grub. They gave us feck all throughout the few days of filming, I mean feck all! End of! One of the DS's came in about 1.45 a.m. and said, 'You may get some sleep now. Big day tomorrow.' Finally, we all jumped into bed, and then would you believe it, 45 minutes later the horrible whoor came in turning on the lights, shouting, 'Right, up yas get!' And I'm thinking, 'Holy fuck, where am I?!'

So we packed our bags, which was a nightmare. The admin killed me, as I wouldn't be good at stuff like that. I've a shite head for that type of stuff, so I was all over the shop all the time. The team were great at helping me, especially Stephanie Roche; she was like my mammy. I've great time for everyone who I went to hell with, but Stephanie was special, what a woman she is. Legend!

On day two we went off to do this thing called 'Scratch'. I had no clue what it was, to be honest, and I think that's a good thing. Ignorance is bliss and all that. I got off to the worst possible start that morning, or should I say middle of the night! We were in such a rush getting our gear ready to head off, because, you see, the DS's come into the room, and just by them standing there, their presence alone puts massive panic in the room.

After we were packed, we jumped on this bus, and it was freezing, which was all part of the plan. They had the air con on full blast so we couldn't sleep. How lousy was that?! All of us sitting there after 45 minutes' sleep, cold and hungry. It was halfway towards the Scratch destination when it dawned on me that I had never taken my heartburn tablet. I take a prescribed pill every morning to keep the heartburn at bay, and I could already feel the ready-made poxy porridge they gave us climbing up my chest and into the back of my throat.

I was afraid to take a sip of water because they check your water bottle before every event, and if it's not full to the tip they make you pour it over your head. I also realised that I had forgotten to take my inhaler with me, and anyone who has asthma knows that when you don't have an inhaler with you, you can actually make yourself dizzy with panic. So because of the poxy heartburn and no inhaler I was in a world of fear. The heartburn got so bad that I simply had to take a sip of water! What I really needed, apart from a few Rennies of course, was a big pint of milk, but sure, unless I jumped off the bus and hopped a local farmer's fence, went into a field and pulled the tits off a cow, there was no hope of me getting my hands on any milk. I wouldn't mind, but the water nearly made things worse!

We eventually got to a beach called Barley Cove at the tip of Cork. After a bit of abuse by the DS's, it wasn't long before I had my bottle of water poured down the back of my neck, and we got going. In Scratch, there is no 'Why', there is just 'Do'. No matter what the DS's tell you to do, you do it or you go home, simple as that. This went on for well over four hours. It was some experience. Just a war, is what it was – madness.

I remember, about 20 minutes in, having battles with myself over having no inhaler and having heartburn until I just said to myself, 'Shut the fuck up, Rory, or go home.' So just like that, I thankfully got 'in the zone', and anyone who trains or plays sport will know what that means. It's a great place to be. I was locked in and ready for anything that was thrown my way. As horrible as it was, I kind of enjoyed it.

Yes, I was one of them who puked and had to put it in my pocket. Sure listen, it was that bonkers that anything went. It was just them DS's doing what they could to break you. We unfortunately lost John Sharpson and Anna Caplice during Scratch, two really great people who were defo missed when they were gone.

I have to say one of the best feelings I had on that show was when Scratch was officially over and we could head back to our bus. I felt on top of the world. It was only a few hours after I'd failed to climb the ship and had felt very low. Now here I was on cloud nine, but sure listen, isn't that life? As Rocky Balboa says, 'It ain't about how hard you hit, it's about how hard you can get hit and keep moving forward.' Just don't give up.

After slogging on a beach in West Cork for nearly five hours, we were on our bus headed to Mizen Head, and do you know what our reward was for completing Scratch, food-wise? It was a Pot Noodle and an apple, and to really rub it in, the water they gave us for the Pot Noodle was lukewarm, so that it didn't cook fully, and was half-crunchy. Rotten!

That's how much they messed with your head all the time, because it's the little things that can break you when you're already half-broken!

As we made our way to Mizen Head, there was a great buzz on the bus while we got our heads around how crazy the Scratch experience was. And then we learned that all we had to do at Mizen Head was fall backwards off the Mizen Head bridge? Grand yeah! I was shitting it, but we all got it done, thank God. I had awful hardship trying to climb back up the side of the drop. My arms were burnt out from Scratch, and my 18-and-a-half-stone frame was not the handiest to get up the cliff. I eventually got myself up, though, with the small help of DS Stafford. The interesting thing about this part was when I was struggling to climb back up and kept falling back down, all I could think of was how useless I must look to the rest of the team.

They were all over on a pier looking at me, and I was thinking, 'Jesus Christ, Rory, another thing you can't do.' It's funny, when we all went back to camp after Mizen Head, a few people came up and said that they found it very inspiring seeing me struggle but eventually get up the cliff. I think that's a perfect example of human self-doubt. We can often look at the negative side of things, but all you have to do to turn that around is take another person's point of view. Most often in life, nobody is harder on you than you are.

One bit of craic we did have around that time was hanging out of a helicopter flying over Mizen Head. That was some experience, and was a perk of doing the show, as I can't imagine the public is allowed to do that. I did it with Darran, which was class. Mind you, dangling from a harness wasn't exactly comfortable for my little pal between my legs, but it was worth the bit of discomfort for the views!

Later that evening we had to go into a building on fire and rescue a couple of very heavy manikins. Without a doubt I found this experience the worst out of all the madness we went through. The heat in that building is hard to describe, and me with the asthma as well. The breathing was all over the shop, it was just brutal. Myself and Niamh Cullen were like two rabbits in headlights, both of us clueless, and the DS's roaring abuse at us from all angles.

God, it was horrible. I think we were in there for about 12 or 13 minutes, but it felt like two days by the time we got the two 'bodies' out. Thankfully, it wasn't a pass/fail event, or we'd have been on our way home. Sure listen, it's all about the experience. Myself and Niamh often laugh about it when we chat to each other. Whatever you do, just don't ring us if your gaff is on fire!

We got into bed at about 2 a.m. on the second night. I had been asleep for about an hour when Darran tapped me to wake me up for night duty. We needed two people guarding the door at all times. I pulled myself out of bed – tired isn't even the word, I was beyond bolloxed – put on my hat and grabbed my bar. They didn't show this, but we had to go everywhere with that bar, and with the hat on. The bar was a heavy enough yoke, but if you got caught without it, then a trip down to the bell was on the cards. This involved running down 170 steps, ringing a bell, and then having 90 seconds to run all the way back up the 170 steps – tough going!

Stephanie Roche was on duty with me, and she had just walked out ahead of me, when I walked out, turned the corner and saw Ray Goggins. 'Oh no,' I managed to say as he grabbed me, turned me around, shoved me against the wall and said, 'You shut your mouth, Number 13!' He then threw a Black Cat banger or a flare or something into the room, and a bang went off and the most freakish music ever came on.

Bedlam is what it was, as all of the rest of the recruits were dragged out of bed and told to strip down to their briefs. 'What the fuck are they going to do now?' I thought to myself, and just like that, we were told to jump into this Arctic-cold well and float around for a minute or so. After that we were ordered up onto the roof, doing push-ups, sit-ups, squats, you name it, all of us in our underwear, soaking wet. It was then that I really knew I was half-mad signing up to this. Gas thing about it is, at least once every hour they ask you if you want to go home, and the answer is always 'No, DS!' Like, how could you be well in the head? But I suppose it was just the buzz and not being willing to give in that would keep you going.

The next day, again after very little sleep and food, we found ourselves on a beach being tortured for ages. Then we walked around the corner and could see a ring made out of sandbags and boxing gloves on the ground. I knew well that this was the combat part, where we had to fight each other! I was kind of looking forward to it, as I would have done plenty of boxing over the years and would be well able to mind myself. But at the same time, I was shitting it, because there were a few animals I might have to fight, and it was going to be shown on national TV a few months later. So there was that nervous energy.

When they called out my number and then Number 7, I was surprised, as it was Peter Stringer. He's half my size, but a complete savage. As we were putting on our gloves there were no words between myself and Pete. We both knew that once the bell went it was hell for leather. It was creeping into my mind that I was about to fight *Peter Stringer*, a legend of Irish rugby who I would have watched for years.

We were instructed that contact was between the neck and the waist. But sure the minute the bell went, Stringer caught me with a jab to the nose, cute whoor. That's experience for you! So I just horsed into him. I got tired after about 45 seconds, and he started to land a few, but thankfully the fight lasted only a minute, because you could slap the head off Pete all day and he'd still come back for more, a real pit bull terrier. I also fought Darran, but the cameras didn't show it. I enjoyed that part of the show, because I like getting stuck in. Some people didn't like it at all, and we lost poor Deric Hartigan during it as he broke a rib. As did Ryan Andrews –

how Ryan managed to get through the whole course with a broken rib is beyond me. A complete beast!

I did one camera interview during them few days, where you are called from your room with a black sack over your head (which is not one bit comfortable) and brought into another room. It's either the DS interrogating you, or it's the production team asking how you're getting on. I found the interrogation part OK, as I was just very honest in my answers and the lads didn't grill me too much. The interview with the camera I did find tough, though, because at this stage the body and mind were exhausted. Barely any sleep, not much food and being tortured defo takes its toll.

During the interview, I could feel myself getting emotional, it's not a nice feeling, especially when the camera is on you, but I couldn't hold back the tears. I was cut right back, and was being very honest about who I am and the struggle I have with not feeling good enough. It took me a couple of minutes before I could even get the words 'mental health' out of my mouth. I was just an emotional wreck, to be honest, and it all came out.

It felt the same as recovering from a three-day stag party, just all over the place, only this time there was no alcohol involved. After that interview, I felt very low, and like I had had enough, and wanted to go home. But it's amazing how a few words at the perfect time can mean the world to people. When the black sack was put back over my head, I was a broken man. But the DS, who I later found out was Rossa O'Donnell, gave me a few words in my ear.

They're not meant to do this, but he felt I needed and deserved them for my efforts to date. He didn't say anything too mad, just that I was doing great, and to keep my head up and keep driving on. I've met Rossa on a few occasions since that, and I always tell him how much those words meant to me. He said he had gone through something similar himself on his selection course many years ago, and a DS had shown him some positive vibes. It had meant the world to him, so he knew it was needed for me. What a great fella!

When I made my way back into the dorm, it was clear I had been crying, big puffy red eyes on me. Everyone was asking if I was OK, and I just said I'd had a tough interview, but that I'd be grand. Little did I know at the time that Ryan Andrews was looking over at me thinking, 'God, if Rory can be like that, the big strong guy in the room, so can I,' and he went on to have a tough interview himself, speaking about his dad struggling very bad with Covid.

But you see, that's OK. It's OK to be honest about your true feelings. Anyone who follows me will know that mental health means a lot to me. It's been a huge part of my journey and still is. I remember the night that interview was aired on TV, I got a lot of messages and feedback. I suppose I was showing people, men especially, that it's OK to show your true emotions, that it doesn't make you weak.

The body and mind were defo starting to go at this stage, and we had to do another pass/fail event, which was on a submarine stuck in the water. I didn't find that too bad, as I knew they couldn't kill us, but it felt like they were going to alright. We were handcuffed to the ground, with water coming up around us, and we were in the water for ages. It was arctic cold.

I got through that, and there were only 10 of us left then. We lost a few great soldiers during that event: Valerie Mulcahy (gas woman, always brings the craic), Niamh Cullen (a dote, and was great at doing stretches and meditation with the team) and Darran. It was tough when Darran went, as we got on so well, the two GAA lads sticking together. I defo missed him in the room after he was gone.

After the water challenge, Ryan Andrews got hypothermia, so we all had to dress him. I remember running over to the bus and leaning into the boot to get his bag, and when I was coming back out, I banged my head off the top of the bus. The adrenaline was high in me at the time because of the buzz of passing the event so I didn't really feel it, but as the next few hours went on, I started to go downhill very quickly. We were all getting ready for a hike that was taking place the following morning, in a few hours, like!

I was going around the room with my head up my hole. I just didn't feel well. I actually felt kind of drunk. Ryan said he was trying to help me pack but that I wasn't making any sense. Then in came Ray Goggins and told us to stand in a square and asked us to pick out who we felt wasn't going to pass the course. It was a dirty thing to have to do, but I knew what they were at. We were a strongly bonded team, and they were trying to break us.

At this stage, I knew deep down that I wouldn't be lasting much longer. I didn't need anyone else to tell me. Sure, everyone was standing upright with their bar in their hands ready for war, and then there was me, standing there swaying with my belly and arse hanging out. I'd say a good fart would have blown me over at that stage.

Two people called me out and said I wouldn't last the course, and sure all I could do at that moment in time was agree with them! I'm surprised more didn't pick me; I was that fucked. I could barely stand, never mind getting through a 20k hike carrying 40 pounds of weight in just a few hours' time – would you stop!

After this, a DS came in and told us to crawl around the room with our bars. Jesus, that was horrible. We only did one lap of the room and it felt like I crawled two laps of Croke Park. When I eventually pulled my beaten body off the dusty ground, I knew I was as good as done!

I stood up and asked Andrew Trimble, who was our captain at the time, to call a DS, as I needed to speak with one. Ray called me out of the room and sat me down. I told him I felt drunk in there and needed to see a doctor. He shined a light into my eyes and told me I was absolutely bolloxed. I told him he wasn't getting my armband. I didn't want to quit, I just wanted to talk to a doctor.

When I went back into the dorm everyone was getting into bed to get their two hours of sleep before the hike. I laid in bed with the spins and dozed off until Ray came over and tapped me on the shoulder and said, 'Come on.' That was the last time I would be in that dorm.

I walked outside and there was the doctor, Jason, a really sound man. He brought me down to his room and I couldn't stop crying. I was never in a worse heap in my life. He told me, 'You need to make the right decision here. You're concussed and basically broken.' So he called in Ray, and we had a really nice chat; it was raw, but I'll never forget it until the day I die. I was in cuckoo-land, but he said some nice things to me that meant a lot, and I gave him my band. At the end of the day, I had given it my all, and to get credit off the likes of Ray Goggins is what that show is all about.

I woke up the following morning in the recovery room in bits from head to toe, but I felt good, felt proud of myself. I remember looking in the mirror and seeing a pale shadow of myself and saying, 'No regrets, Rory. Ya hear me? No regrets.' I did it so that over the next few days and weeks, when the body and mind recovered, I wouldn't be beating myself up over not passing the course. I had emptied the tank, and that's all any of us can do.

I did my closing interview – a few laughs, a few tears – and made my way back to the hotel in Cork. A few of my fellow recruits were still there, and I had breakfast with them, and what a laugh we had, thinking of all the madness we had just gone through. Such a bond I'll have forever more with these people, just great folk. Proper solid. I have to mention Peter, Ryan and Marc O'Neill for passing the course, what hardy whoors and great men they are. A special mention as well for former Olympian swimmer Melanie Nocher, who got through that hike. What a tough woman, and the mammy of the group.

It was a once-in-a-lifetime experience doing *Hell Week*, and the positive messages I received from the public was insane! I still to this day haven't got back to read half of them. If you were one who sent a message, thanks very much, I appreciate it, and I hope my journey on that show helped some people with their own life journey, because at the end of the day, *Hell Week* was like life – there are ups and downs, high and lows, but you keep moving forward.

# Conclusion

Now that we thankfully seem to have passed the crazy lockdown and restrictions of the coronavirus, it's important to try to look back at some of the positives of it (positives, says you, would you stop!). But seriously, there were some upsides, especially those early days of lockdown, when the whole world had no choice but to slow down.

Many people got the chance to spend quality time with their family: parents who might have been working around the clock 24/7 before the pandemic got time to chill out and enjoy themselves with their kids. And, for some, it provided a much-needed chance to see what is most important in this world. It gave us valuable perspective to have in our back pockets going forward with life.

Whenever things are bogging you down, try to think of the days when we couldn't go further than 2km from our house; you couldn't visit relatives or friends and you couldn't shake hands or hug anyone without feeling uncomfortable! You see, everyone built resilience during the pandemic without even realising it – so be proud of that and look forward to the future with hope and promise. In the words of the great Dermot Kennedy, better days are coming, if no one told you ...